Applications regarding translation rights in any
work by Aldous Huxley should be addressed
to Chatto & Windus, 40 William IV Street,
London, W.C. 2

ALDOUS HUXLEY

*

On the Margin

By ALDOUS HUXLEY

Novels

CROME YELLOW
ANTIC HAY
THOSE BARREN LEAVES
POINT COUNTER POINT
BRAVE NEW WORLD
EYELESS IN GAZA
AFTER MANY A SUMMER
TIME MUST HAVE A STOP
APE AND ESSENCE
THE GENIUS AND THE GODDESS*

Short Stories

LIMBO
MORTAL COILS
LITTLE MEXICAN
TWO OR THREE GRACES
BRIEF CANDLES

Biography

GREY EMINENCE
THE DEVILS OF LOUDUN*

Essays and Belles Lettres

ON THE MARGIN
ALONG THE ROAD
PROPER STUDIES
DO WHAT YOU WILL
MUSIC AT NIGHT &
VULGARITY IN LITERATURE
TEXTS AND PRETEXTS (Anthology)
THE OLIVE TREE
ENDS AND MEANS (An Enquiry
into the Nature of Ideals)
THE ART OF SEEING*
THEMES AND VARIATIONS
THE PERENNIAL PHILOSOPHY*
SCIENCE, LIBERTY AND PEACE*
THE DOORS OF PERCEPTION*
HEAVEN AND HELL*
ADONIS AND THE ALPHABET*

Travel

JESTING PILATE (Illustrated)
BEYOND THE MEXIQUE BAY (Illustrated)

Poetry and Drama

VERSES AND A COMEDY
(including early poems, Leda, The Cicadas
and The World of Light, a Comedy)
THE GIOCONDA SMILE*

Not yet available in this Collected Edition

ALDOUS HUXLEY

On the Margin

Notes and Essays

1956

Chatto & Windus

LONDON

PUBLISHED BY
Chatto & Windus Ltd
LONDON

✱

Clarke, Irwin & Company Ltd
TORONTO

FIRST PUBLISHED 1923
FIRST ISSUED IN THIS COLLECTED
EDITION 1948
REPRINTED 1956
PRINTED IN GREAT BRITAIN

CONTENTS

NOTE

MOST of these essays appeared in *The Athenæum* under the title MARGINALIA and over the signature AUTOLYCUS. The others were first printed in *The Weekly Westminster Gazette*, *The London Mercury*, and *Vanity Fair* (New York).

CENTENARIES

FROM Bocca di Magra to Bocca d'Arno, mile after mile, the sandy beaches smoothly, unbrokenly extend. Inland from the beach, behind a sheltering belt of pines, lies a strip of coastal plain— flat as a slice of Holland and dyked with slow streams. Corn grows here and the vine, with plantations of slim poplars interspersed, and fat water-meadows. Here and there the streams brim over into shallow lakes, whose shores are fringed with sodden fields of rice. And behind this strip of plain, four or five miles from the sea, the mountains rise, suddenly and steeply : the Apuan Alps. Their highest crests are of bare limestone, streaked here and there with the white marble which brings prosperity to the little towns that stand at their feet : Massa and Carrara, Serravezza, Pietrasanta. Half the world's tombstones are scooped out of these noble crags. Their lower slopes are grey with olive trees, green with woods of chestnut. Over their summits repose the enormous sculptured masses of the clouds.

From cape to cape, with a bridge-like shape,
  Over a torrent sea,
Sunbeam-proof, I hang like a roof,—
  The mountains its columns be.

ON THE MARGIN

The landscape fairly quotes Shelley at you. This sea with its luminous calms and sudden tempests, these dim blue islands hull down on the horizon, these mountains and their marvellous clouds, these rivers and woodlands are the very substance of his poetry. Live on this coast for a little and you will find yourself constantly thinking of that lovely, that strangely childish poetry, that beautiful and child-like man. Perhaps his spirit haunts the coast. It was in this sea that he sailed his flimsy boat, steering with one hand and holding in the other his little volume of Æschylus. You picture him so on the days of calm. And on the days of sudden violent storm you think of him, too. The lightnings cut across the sky, the thunders are like terrible explosions overhead, the squall comes down with a fury. What news of the flimsy boat ? None, save only that a few days after the storm a young body is washed ashore, battered, unrecognizable ; the little Æschylus in the coat pocket is all that tells us that this was Shelley.

I have been spending the summer on this haunted coast. That must be my excuse for mentioning in so self-absorbed a world as is ours the name of a poet who has been dead these hundred years. But be reassured. I have no intention of writing an article about the ineffectual angel beating in the void his something-or-other wings in vain. I do not mean to add my croak to the mellifluous chorus of centenary celebrators. No; the ghost of Shelley, who walks in Versilia and the Lunigia, by the shores of the Gulf of Spezia and below Pisa where Arno disembogues, this ghost with whom I have shaken hands and talked, incites me, not to add a supererogatory and impertinent encomium, but rather to protest against the outpourings of the other encomiasts, of the honey-voiced centenary-chanters.

The cooing of these persons, ordinarily a specific against insomnia, is in this case an irritant ; it rouses, it exacerbates. For annoying and disgusting it certainly is, this spectacle of a rebellious youth praised to fulsomeness, a hundred years after his death, by people who would hate him and be horrified by him, if he were alive, as much as the Scotch reviewers hated and were horrified by Shelley. How would these persons treat

3

a young contemporary who, not content with being a literary innovator, should use his talent to assault religion and the established order, should blaspheme against plutocracy and patriotism, should proclaim himself a Bolshevik, an internationalist, a pacifist, a conscientious objector ? They would say of him that he was a dangerous young man who ought to be put in his place ; and they would either disparage and denigrate his talent, or else—if they were a little more subtly respectable—they would never allow his name to get into print in any of the periodicals which they controlled.

But seeing that Shelley was safely burnt on the sands of Viareggio a hundred years ago, seeing that he is no longer a live dangerous man but only a dead classic, these respectable supporters of established literature and established society join in chorus to praise him, and explain his meaning, and preach sermons over him. The mellifluous cooing is accompanied by a snuffle, and there hangs over these centenary celebrations a genial miasma of hypocrisy and insincerity. The effect of these festal anniversaries in England is not to rekindle

life in the great dead; a centenary is
rather a second burial, a reaffirmation
of deadness. A spirit that was once
alive is fossilized and, in the midst of
solemn and funereal ceremonies, the
petrified classic is duly niched in the
temple of respectability.

How much better they order these
things in Italy ! In that country—which
one must ever admire more the more one
sees of it—they duly celebrate their
great men ; but celebrate them not
with a snuffle, not in black clothes, not
with prayer-books in their hands, crape
round their hats, and a hatred, in their
hearts, of all that has to do with life and
vigour. No, no ; they make their dead
an excuse for quickening life among the
living ; they get fun out of their centenaries.

Last year the Italians were celebrating
the six hundredth anniversary of Dante's
death. Now, imagine what this celebration would have been like in England.
All the oldest critics and all the young
men who aspire to be old would have
written long articles in all the literary
papers. That would have set the tone.
After that some noble lord, or even

a Prince of the Blood, would have un-
veiled a monument designed by Frampton
or some other monumental mason of the
Academy. Imbecile speeches in words
of not more than two syllables would
then have been pronounced over the
ashes of the world's most intelligent
poet. To his intelligence no reference
would, of course, be made ; but his
character, ah ! his character would get
a glowing press. The most fiery and
bitter of men would be held up as an
example to all Sunday-school children.

After this display of reverence, we
should have had a lovely historical pageant
in the rain. A young female dressed in
white bunting would have represented
Beatrice, and for the Poet himself some
actor manager with a profile and a voice
would have been found. Guelfs and
Ghibellines in fancy dress of the period
would go splashing about in the mud,
and a great many verses by Louis Napoleon
Parker would be declaimed. And at the
end we should all go home with colds
in our heads and suffering from septic
ennui, but with, at the same time, a
pleasant feeling of virtuousness, as though
we had been at church.

CENTENARIES

See now what happens in Italy. The principal event in the Dante celebration is an enormous military review. Hundreds of thousands of wiry little brown men parade the streets of Florence. Young officers of a fabulous elegance clank along in superbly tailored riding breeches and glittering top-boots. The whole female population palpitates. It is an excellent beginning. Speeches are then made, as only in Italy they can be made — round, rumbling, sonorous speeches, all about Dante the Italianissimous poet, Dante the irredentist, Dante the prophet of Greater Italy, Dante the scourge of Jugo-Slavs and Serbs. Immense enthusiasm. Never having read a line of his works, we feel that Dante is our personal friend, a brother Fascist.

After that the real fun begins ; we have the *manifestazioni sportive* of the centenary celebrations. Innumerable bicycle races are organized. Fierce young Fascisti with the faces of Roman heroes pay their homage to the Poet by doing a hundred and eighty kilometres to the hour round the Circuit of Milan. High speed Fiats and Ansaldos and Lancias race one another across the

Apennines and round the bastions of the Alps. Pigeons are shot, horses gallop, football is played under the broiling sun. Long live Dante !

How infinitely preferable this is to the stuffiness and the snuffle of an English centenary ! Poetry, after all, is life, not death. Bicycle races may not have very much to do with Dante—though I can fancy him, his thin face set like metal, whizzing down the spirals of Hell on a pair of twinkling wheels or climbing laboriously the one-in-three gradients of Purgatory Mountain on the back of his trusty Sunbeam. No, they may not have much to do with Dante ; but pageants in Anglican cathedral closes, boring articles by old men who would hate and fear him if he were alive, speeches by noble lords over monuments made by Royal Academicians—these, surely, have even less to do with the author of the *Inferno*.

It is not merely their great dead whom the Italians celebrate in this gloriously living fashion. Even their religious festivals have the same jovial warm-blooded character. This summer, for example, a great feast took place at

CENTENARIES

Loreto to celebrate the arrival of a new image of the Virgin to replace the old one which was burnt some little while ago. The excitement started in Rome, where the image, after being blessed by the Pope, was taken in a motor-car to the station amid cheering crowds who shouted, "Evviva Maria" as the Fiat and its sacred burden rolled past. The arrival of the Virgin in Loreto was the signal for a tremendous outburst of jollification. The usual bicycle races took place; there were football matches and pigeon - shooting competitions and Olympic games. The fun lasted for days. At the end of the festivities two cardinals went up in aeroplanes and blessed the assembled multitudes — an incident of which the Pope is said to have remarked that the blessing, in this case, did indeed come from heaven.

Rare people! If only we Anglo-Saxons could borrow from the Italians some of their realism, their love of life for its own sake, of palpable, solid, immediate things. In this dim land of ours we are accustomed to pay too much respect to fictitious values; we worship invisibilities and in our enjoyment of

immediate life we are restrained by
imaginary inhibitions. We think too
much of the past, of metaphysics, of
tradition, of the ideal future, of decorum and good form ; too little of life
and the glittering noisy moment. The
Italians are born Futurists. It did not
need Marinetti to persuade them to
celebrate Dante with bicycle races ; they
would have done it naturally, spontan-
eously, if no Futurist propaganda had
ever been issued. Marinetti is the product of modern Italy, not modern Italy
of Marinetti. They are all Futurists
in that burningly living Italy where
we from the North seek only an escape
into the past. Or rather, they are not
Futurists : Marinetti's label was badly
chosen. They are Presentists. The early
Christians preoccupied with nothing but
the welfare of their souls in the life to
come were Futurists, if you like.

We shall do well to learn something
of their lively Presentism. Let us hope
that our great-grandchildren will celebrate the next centenary of Shelley's
death by aerial regattas and hydroplane
races. The living will be amused and
the dead worthily commemorated. The

spirit of the man who delighted, during life, in wind and clouds, in mountain-tops and waters, in the flight of birds and the gliding of ships, will be rejoiced when young men celebrate his memory by flying through the air or skimming, like alighting swans, over the surface of the sea.

The rocks are cloven, and through the purple night
I see cars drawn by rainbow-winged steeds
Which trample the dim winds ; in each there stands
A wild-eyed charioteer urging their flight.
Some look behind, as fiends pursued them there,
And yet I see no shapes but the keen stars ;
Others, with burning eyes, lean forth, and drink
With eager lips the wind of their own speed,
As if the thing they loved fled on before,
And now, even now, they clasped it.

The man who wrote this is surely more suitably celebrated by aeroplane or even bicycle races than by seven-column articles from the pens of Messrs.—well, perhaps we had better mention no names. Let us take a leaf out of the Italian book.

11

ON RE-READING "CANDIDE"

THE furniture vans had unloaded their freight in the new house. We were installed, or, at least, we were left to make the best of an unbearable life in the dirt and the confusion. One of the Pre-Raphaelites, I forget at the moment which, once painted a picture called " The Last Day in the Old Home." A touching subject. But it would need a grimmer, harder brush to depict the horrors of " The First Day in the New Home." I had sat down in despair among the tumbled movables when I noticed—with what a thrill of pleased recognition—the top of a little leather-bound book protruding from among a mass of bulkier volumes in an uncovered case. It was *Candide*, my treasured little first edition of 1759, with its discreetly ridiculous title-page, " *Candide ou L'Optimisme*, Traduit de l'Allemand de Mr. le Docteur Ralph."

Optimism—I had need of a little at the moment, and as Mr. le Docteur Ralph is notoriously one of the preachers most capable of inspiring it, I took up the volume and began to read : " Il y avait en Westphalie, dans le Château de

ON RE-READING *CANDIDE*

Mr. le Baron de Thunder-ten-tronckh. . . ."
I did not put down the volume till I had
reached the final : " Il faut cultiver
notre jardin." I felt the wiser and
the more cheerful for Doctor Ralph's
ministrations.

But the remarkable thing about re-
reading *Candide* is not that the book
amuses one, not that it delights and
astonishes with its brilliance ; that is
only to be expected. No, it evokes a
new and, for me at least, an unanticipated
emotion. In the good old days, before
the Flood, the history of Candide's
adventures seemed to us quiet, sheltered,
middle-class people only a delightful
phantasy, or at best a high-spirited
exaggeration of conditions which we
knew, vaguely and theoretically, to exist,
to have existed, a long way off in space
and time. But read the book to-day ;
you feel yourself entirely at home in its
pages. It is like reading a record of
the facts and opinions of 1922 ; nothing
was ever more applicable, more completely to the point. The world in
which we live is recognizably the world
of Candide and Cunégonde, of Martin
and the Old Woman who was a Pope's

daughter and the betrothed of the sovereign Prince of Massa-Carrara. The only difference is that the horrors crowd rather more thickly on the world of 1922 than they did on Candide's world. The manœuvrings of Bulgare and Abare, the intestine strife in Morocco, the earthquake and *auto-da-fé* are but pale poor things compared with the Great War, the Russian Famine, the Black and Tans, the Fascisti, and all the other horrors of which we can proudly boast. " Quand Sa Hautesse envoye un vaisseau en Egypte," remarked the Dervish, " s'embarrasse-t-elle si les souris qui sont dans le vaisseau sont à leur aise ou non ? " No ; but there are moments when Sa Hautesse, absent-mindedly no doubt, lets fall into the hold of the vessel a few dozen of hungry cats ; the present seems to be one of them.

Cats in the hold ? There is nothing in that to be surprised at. The wisdom of Martin and the Old Woman who was once betrothed to the Prince of Massa-Carrara has become the everyday wisdom of all the world since 1914. In the happy Victorian and Edwardian past, Western Europe, like Candide, was surprised at

14

everything. It was amazed by the frightful conduct of King Bomba, amazed by the Turks, amazed by the political chicanery and loose morals of the Second Empire—(what is all Zola but a prolonged exclamation of astonishment at the goings-on of his contemporaries ?). After that we were amazed at the disgusting behaviour of the Boers, while the rest of Europe was amazed at ours. There followed the widespread astonishment that in this, the so-called twentieth century, black men should be treated as they were being treated on the Congo and the Amazon. Then came the war : a great outburst of indignant astonishment, and afterwards an acquiescence as complete, as calmly cynical as Martin's. For we have discovered, in the course of the somewhat excessively prolonged *histoire à la Candide* of the last seven years, that astonishment is a supererogatory emotion. All things are possible, not merely for Providence, whose ways we had always known, albeit for some time rather theoretically, to be strange, but also for men.

Men, we thought, had grown up from the brutal and rampageous hobbledehoyism of earlier ages and were now as polite and genteel as Gibbon himself. We now know better. Create a hobble-dehoy environment and you will have hobbledehoy behaviour ; create a Gibbonish environment and every one will be, more or less, genteel. It seems obvious, now. And now that we are living in a hobbledehoy world, we have learnt Martin's lesson so well that we can look on almost unmoved at the most appalling natural catastrophes and at exhibitions of human stupidity and wickedness which would have aroused us in the past to surprise and indignation. Indeed, we have left Martin behind and are become, with regard to many things, Pococurante.

And what is the remedy ? Mr. le Docteur Ralph would have us believe that it consists in the patient cultivation of our gardens. He is probably right. The only trouble is that the gardens of some of us seem hardly worth cultivating. The garden of the bank clerk and the factory hand, the shop-girl's garden, the garden of the civil servant and the politician—can one cultivate them with much enthusiasm ? Or, again, there is my garden, the garden of literary journalism. In this little plot I dig and delve, plant, prune, and finally reap—sparsely enough, goodness knows !— from one year's end to another. And to what purpose, to whom for a good, as the Latin Grammar would say ? Ah, there you have me.

There is a passage in one of Tchekov's letters which all literary journalists should inscribe in letters of gold upon their writing desks. " I send you," says Tchekov to his correspondent, " Mihail-ovsky's article on Tolstoy. . . . It's a good article, but it's strange : one might write a thousand such articles and things would not be one step forwarder, and it would still remain unintelligible why such articles are written."

Il faut cultiver notre jardin. Yes, but suppose one begins to wonder why ?

ACCIDIE

THE cœnobites of the Thebaid were subjected to the assaults of many demons. Most of these evil spirits came furtively with the coming of night. But there was one, a fiend of deadly subtlety, who was not afraid to walk by day. The holy men of the desert called him the *dæmon meridianus*; for his favourite hour of visitation was in the heat of the day. He would lie in wait for monks grown weary with working in the oppressive heat, seizing a moment of weakness to force an entrance into their hearts. And once installed there, what havoc he wrought! For suddenly it would seem to the poor victim that the day was intolerably long and life desolatingly empty. He would go to the door of his cell and look up at the sun and ask himself if a new Joshua had arrested it midway up the heavens. Then he would go back into the shade and wonder what good he was doing in that cell or if there was any object in existence. Then he would look at the sun again and find it indubitably stationary, and the hour of the communal repast of the evening as remote as ever. And he would go back to his meditations, to sink, sink through disgust and lassitude into the black depths of despair and hopeless unbelief. When that happened the demon smiled and took his departure, conscious that he had done a good morning's work.

Throughout the Middle Ages this demon was known as Acedia, or, in English, Accidie. Monks were still his favourite victims, but he made many conquests among the laity also. Along with *gastrimargia, fornicatio, philargyria, tristitia, cenodoxia, ira* and *superbia, acedia* or *tædium cordis* is reckoned as one of the eight principal vices to which man is subject. Inaccurate psychologists of evil are wont to speak of accidie as though it were plain sloth. But sloth is only one of the numerous manifestations of the subtle and complicated vice of accidie. Chaucer's discourse on it in the " Parson's Tale " contains a very precise description of this disastrous vice of the spirit. " Accidie," he tells us, " makith a man hevy, thoghtful and wrawe." It paralyses human will, " it forsloweth and forsluggeth " a man whenever he attempts to act. From accidie comes dread to begin to work any good deeds, and finally wanhope, or despair. On its way to ultimate wanhope, accidie produces a whole crop of minor sins, such as idleness, tardiness, *lâchesse*, coldness, undevotion and " the synne of worldly sorrow, such as is cleped *tristitia*, that sleth man, as seith seint Poule." Those who have sinned by accidie find their everlasting home in the fifth circle of the Inferno. They are plunged in the same black bog with the Wrathful, and their sobs and words come bubbling up to the surface :

Fitti nel limo dicon : " Tristi fummo
  nell' aer dolce che dal sol s' allegra,
  portando dentro accidioso fummo ;

Or ci attristiam nella belletta negra."
  Quest' inno si gorgoglian nella strozza,
  chè dir nol posson con parola integra.

Accidie did not disappear with the monasteries and the Middle Ages. The Renaissance was also subject to it. We find a copious description of the symptoms of acedia in Burton's *Anatomy of Melancholy*. The results of the midday demon's machinations are now known as the vapours or the spleen. To the spleen amiable Mr. Matthew Green, of the

ACCIDIE

Custom House, devoted those eight
hundred octosyllables which are his claim
to immortality. For him it is a mere
disease to be healed by temperate diet :

> Hail ! water gruel, healing power,
> Of easy access to the poor ;

by laughter, reading and the company of
unaffected young ladies :

> Mothers, and guardian aunts, forbear
> Your impious pains to form the fair,
> Nor lay out so much cost and art
> But to deflower the virgin heart ;

by the avoidance of party passion, drink,
Dissenters and missionaries, especially mis-
sionaries : to whose undertakings Mr.
Green always declined to subscribe :

> I laugh off spleen and keep my pence
> From spoiling Indian innocence ;

by refraining from going to law, writing
poetry and thinking about one's future
state.

The Spleen was published in the 'thirties
of the eighteenth century. Accidie was
still, if not a sin, at least a disease. But
a change was at hand. " The sin of
worldly sorrow, such as is cleped *tristitia*,"
became a literary virtue, a spiritual mode.

The apostles of melancholy wound their
faint horns, and the Men of Feeling
wept. Then came the nineteenth century
and romanticism ; and with them the
triumph of the meridian demon. Accidie
in its most complicated and most deadly
form, a mixture of boredom, sorrow and
despair, was now an inspiration to the
greatest poets and novelists, and it has
remained so to this day. The Romantics
called this horrible phenomenon the
mal du siècle. But the name made no
difference ; the thing was still the same.
The meridian demon had good cause to
be satisfied during the nineteenth century,
for it was then, as Baudelaire puts it, that

> L'Ennui, fruit de la morne incuriosité,
> Prit les proportions de l'immortalité.

It is a very curious phenomenon, this
progress of accidie from the position of
being a deadly sin, deserving of damna-
tion, to the position first of a disease
and finally of an essentially lyrical emotion,
fruitful in the inspiration of much of the
most characteristic modern literature.
The sense of universal futility, the feelings
of boredom and despair, with the complementary desire to be " anywhere, any-

where out of the world," or at least out
of the place in which one happens at
the moment to be, have been the inspiration of poetry and the novel for a
century and more. It would have been
inconceivable in Matthew Green's day
to have written a serious poem about
ennui. By Baudelaire's time ennui was
as suitable a subject for lyric poetry
as love ; and accidie is still with us as
an inspiration, one of the most serious
and poignant of literary themes. What
is the significance of this fact ? For
clearly the progress of accidie is a spiritual
event of considerable importance. How
is it to be explained ?

It is not as though the nineteenth century invented accidie. Boredom, hope-
lessness and despair have always existed,
and have been felt as poignantly in the
past as we feel them now. Something
has happened to make these emotions
respectable and avowable ; they are no
longer sinful, no longer regarded as the
mere symptoms of disease. That something that has happened is surely simply
history since 1789. The failure of the
French Revolution and the more spec-
tacular downfall of Napoleon planted

accidie in the heart of every youth of the Romantic generation—and not in France alone, but all over Europe—who believed in liberty or whose adolescence had been intoxicated by the ideas of glory and genius. Then came industrial progress with its prodigious multiplication of filth, misery, and ill-gotten wealth ; the defilement of nature by modern industry was in itself enough to sadden many sensitive minds. The discovery that political enfranchisement, so long and stubbornly fought for, was the merest futility and vanity so long as industrial servitude remained in force was another of the century's horrible disillusionments.

A more subtle cause of the prevalence of boredom was the disproportionate growth of the great towns. Habituated to the feverish existence of these few centres of activity, men found that life outside them was intolerably insipid. And at the same time they became so much exhausted by the restlessness of city life that they pined for the monotonous boredom of the provinces, for exotic islands, even for other worlds—any haven of rest. And finally, to crown

ACCIDIE

this vast structure of failures and disillusionments, there came the appalling
catastrophe of the War of 1914. Other
epochs have witnessed disasters, have had
to suffer disillusionment ; but in no century have the disillusionments followed
on one another's heels with such un-
intermitted rapidity as in the twentieth,
for the good reason that in no century
has change been so rapid and so profound.
The *mal du siècle* was an inevitable evil ;
indeed, we can claim with a certain
pride that we have a right to our accidie.
With us it is not a sin or a disease of the
hypochondries ; it is a state of mind
which fate has forced upon us.

SUBJECT-MATTER
OF POETRY

IT should theoretically be possible to make poetry out of anything whatsoever of which the spirit of man can take cognizance. We find, however, as a matter of historical fact, that most of the world's best poetry has been content with a curiously narrow range of subject-matter. The poets have claimed as their domain only a small province of our universe. One of them now and then, more daring or better equipped than the rest, sets out to extend the boundaries of the kingdom. But for the most part the poets do not concern themselves with fresh conquests ; they prefer to consolidate their power at home, enjoying quietly their hereditary possessions. All the world is potentially theirs, but they do not take it. What is the reason for this, and why is it that poetical practice does not conform to critical theory ? The problem has a peculiar relevance and importance in these days, when young poetry claims absolute liberty to speak how it likes of whatsoever it pleases.

Wordsworth, whose literary criticism,

dry and forbidding though its aspect
may be, is always illumined by a penetrating intelligence, Wordsworth touched
upon this problem in his preface to
Lyrical Ballads—touched on it and, as
usual, had something of value to say
about it. He is speaking here of the
most important and the most interesting
of the subjects which may, theoretically,
be made into poetry, but which have, as
a matter of fact, rarely or never under-
gone the transmutation : he is speaking
of the relations between poetry and that
vast world of abstractions and ideas—
science and philosophy—into which so
few poets have ever penetrated. " The
remotest discoveries of the chemist, the
botanist, or mineralogist, will be as
proper objects of the poet's art as any
upon which he is now employed, if the
time should ever come when these things
shall be familiar to us, and the relations
under which they are contemplated shall
be manifestly and palpably material to
us as enjoying and suffering beings."
It is a formidable sentence ; but read
it well, read the rest of the passage from
which it is taken, and you will find it to
be full of critical truth.

The gist of Wordsworth's argument is this. All subjects—" the remotest discoveries of the chemist " are but one example of an unlikely poetic theme—can serve the poet with material for his art, on one condition : that he, and to a lesser degree his audience, shall be able to apprehend the subject with a certain emotion. The subject must somehow be involved in the poet's intimate being before he can turn it into poetry. It is not enough, for example, that he should apprehend it merely through his senses. (The poetry of pure sensation, of sounds and bright colours, is common enough nowadays ; but amusing as we may find it for the moment, it cannot hold the interest for long.) It is not enough, at the other end of the scale, if he apprehends his subject in a purely intellectual manner. An abstract idea must be felt with a kind of passion, it must mean something emotionally significant, it must be as immediate and important to the poet as a personal relationship before he can make poetry of it. Poetry, in a word, must be written by " enjoying and suffering beings," not by beings exclusively dowered with sensations or, as exclusively, with intellect.

Wordsworth's criticism helps us to understand why so few subjects have ever been made into poetry when everything under the sun, and beyond it, is theoretically suitable for transmutation into a work of art. Death, love, religion, nature ; the primary emotions and the ultimate personal mysteries—these form the subject-matter of most of the greatest poetry. And for obvious reasons. These things are " manifestly and palpably material to us as enjoying and suffering beings." But to most men, including the generality of poets, abstractions and ideas are not immediately and passionately moving. They are not enjoying or suffering when they apprehend these things— only thinking.

The men who do feel passionately about abstractions, the men to whom ideas are as persons—moving and disquietingly alive—are very seldom poets. They are men of science and philosophers, preoccupied with the search for truth and not, like the poet, with the expression and creation of beauty. It is very rarely that we find a poet who combines the

power and the desire to express himself
with that passionate apprehension of
ideas and that passionate curiosity about
strange remote facts which characterize
the man of science and the philosopher.
If he possessed the requisite sense of
language and the impelling desire to express himself in terms of beauty, Einstein could write the most intoxicating
lyrics about relativity and the pleasures
of pure mathematics. And if, say, Mr.
Yeats understood the Einstein theory—
which, in company with most other
living poets, he presumably does not,
any more than the rest of us—if he
apprehended it exultingly as something
bold and profound, something vitally
important and marvellously true, he too
could give us, out of the Celtic twilight,
his lyrics of relativity. It is those dis-
tressing little " ifs " that stand in the
way of this happy consummation. The
conditions upon which any but the most
immediately and obviously moving subjects can be made into poetry are so
rarely fulfilled, the combination of poet
and man of science, poet and philosopher, is so uncommon, that the
theoretical universality of the art has

only very occasionally been realized in practice.

Contemporary poetry in the whole of the Western world is insisting, loudly and emphatically through the mouths of its propagandists, on an absolute liberty to speak of what it likes, how it likes. Nothing could be better ; all that we can now ask is that the poets should put the theory into practice, and that they should make use of the liberty which they claim by enlarging the bounds of poetry.

The propagandists would have us believe that the subject-matter of contemporary poetry is new and startling, that modern poets are doing something which has not been done before. " Most of the poets represented in these pages," writes Mr. Louis Untermeyer in his *Anthology of Modern American Poetry*, " have found a fresh and vigorous material in a world of honest and often harsh reality. They respond to the spirit of their times ; not only have their views changed, their vision has been widened to include things unknown to the poets of yesterday. They have learned to distinguish real beauty from mere pretti-

31

ness, to wring loveliness out of squalor, to find wonder in neglected places, to search for hidden truths even in the dark caves of the unconscious." Translated into practice this means that contemporary poets can now write, in the words of Mr. Sandburg, of the " harr and boom of the blast fires," of " wops and bohunks." It means, in fact, that they are at liberty to do what Homer did— to write freely about the immediately moving facts of everyday life. Where Homer wrote of horses and the tamers of horses, our contemporaries write of trains, automobiles, and the various species of wops and bohunks who control the horse-power. That is all. Much too much stress has been laid on the newness of the new poetry ; its newness is simply a return from the jewelled exquisiteness of the eighteen-nineties to the facts and feelings of ordinary life. There is nothing intrinsically novel or surprising in the introduction into poetry of machinery and industrialism, of labour unrest and modern psychology : these things belong to us, they affect us daily as enjoying and suffering beings ; they are a part of our lives, just as the kings, the warriors, the horses and chariots, the picturesque mythology were part of Homer's life. The subject-matter of the new poetry remains the same as that of the old. The old boundaries have not been extended. There would be real novelty in the new poetry if it had, for example, taken to itself any of the new ideas and astonishing facts with which the new science has endowed the modern world. There would be real novelty in it if it had worked out a satisfactory artistic method for dealing with abstractions. It has not. Which simply means that that rare phenomenon, the poet in whose mind ideas are a passion and a personal moving force, does not happen to have appeared.

And how rarely in all the long past he has appeared ! There was Lucretius, the greatest of all the philosophic and scientific poets. In him the passionate apprehension of ideas, and the desire and ability to give them expression, combined to produce that strange and beautiful epic of thought which is without parallel in the whole history of literature. There was Dante, in whose soul the mediæval Christian philosophy was a force that shaped and directed every feeling, thought and action. There was Goethe, who focused into beautiful expression an enormous diffusion of knowledge and ideas. And there the list of the great poets of thought comes to an end. In their task of extending the boundaries of poetry into the remote and abstract world of ideas, they have had a few lesser assistants—Donne, for example, a poet only just less than the greatest; Fulke Greville, that strange, dark-spirited Elizabethan; John Davidson, who made a kind of poetry out of Darwinism; and, most interesting poetical interpreter of nineteenth-century science, Jules Laforgue.

Which of our contemporaries can claim to have extended the bounds of poetry to any material extent? It is not enough to have written about locomotives and telephones, "wops and bohunks," and all the rest of it. That is not extending the range of poetry; it is merely asserting its right to deal with the immediate facts of contemporary life, as Homer and as Chaucer did. The critics who would have us believe that there is something essentially unpoetical about a bohunk (whatever a Bohunk may be), and something essentially poetical about Sir Lancelot of the Lake, are, of course, simply negligible ; they may be dismissed as contemptuously as we have dismissed the pseudo-classical critics who opposed the freedoms of the Romantic Revival. And the critics who think it very new and splendid to bring bohunks into poetry are equally old-fashioned in their ideas.

It will not be unprofitable to compare the literary situation in this early twentieth century of ours with the literary situation of the early seventeenth century. In both epochs we see a reaction against a rich and somewhat formalized poetical tradition expressing itself in a determination to extend the range of subject-matter, to get back to real life, and to use more natural forms of expression. The difference between the two epochs lies in the fact that the twentieth-century revolution has been the product of a number of minor poets, none of them quite powerful enough to achieve what he theoretically meant to do, while the seventeenth-century revolution was the work of a single poet of genius, John Donne. Donne substituted for the rich formalism of non-dramatic Elizabethan poetry a completely realized new style, the style of the so-called metaphysical poetry of the seventeenth century. He was a poet-philosopher-man-of-action whose passionate curiosity about facts enabled him to make poetry out of the most unlikely aspects of material life, and whose passionate apprehension of ideas enabled him to extend the bounds of poetry beyond the frontiers of common life and its emotions into the void of intellectual abstraction. He put the whole life and the whole mind of his age into poetry.

We to-day are metaphysicals without our Donne. Theoretically we are free to make poetry of everything in the universe ; in practice we are kept within the old limits, for the simple reason that no great man has appeared to show us how we can use our freedom. A certain amount of the life of the twentieth century is to be found in our poetry, but precious little of its mind. We have no poet to-day like that strange old Dean of St. Paul's three hundred years ago—no poet who can skip from the heights of scholastic philosophy to the heights of carnal passion, from the contemplation of divinity to the contemplation of a flea, from the rapt examination of self to an enumeration of the most remote external facts of science, and make all, by his strangely passionate apprehension, into an intensely lyrical poetry.

The few poets who do try to make of contemporary ideas the substance of their poetry, do it in a manner which brings little conviction or satisfaction to the reader. There is Mr. Noyes, who is writing four volumes of verse about the human side of science—in his case, alas, all too human. Then there is Mr. Conrad Aiken. He perhaps is the most successful exponent in poetry of contemporary ideas. In his case, it is clear, " the remotest discoveries of the chemist " are apprehended with a certain passion ; all his emotions are tinged by his ideas. The trouble with Mr. Aiken is that his emotions are apt to degenerate into a kind of intellectual sentimentality, which expresses itself only too easily in his prodigiously fluent, highly coloured verse.

One could lengthen the list of more or less interesting poets who have tried in recent times to extend the boundaries of their art. But one would not find among them a single poet of real importance, not one great or outstanding personality. The twentieth century still awaits its Lucretius, awaits its own philosophical Dante, its new Goethe, its Donne, even its up-to-date Laforgue. Will they appear ? Or are we to go on producing a poetry in which there is no more than the dimmest reflection of that busy and incessant intellectual life which is the characteristic and distinguishing mark of this age ?

WATER MUSIC

THE house in which I live is haunted by the noise of dripping water. Always, day and night, summer and winter, something is dripping somewhere. For many months an unquiet cistern kept up within its iron bosom a long, hollow-toned soliloquy. Now it is mute; but a new and more formidable drip has come into existence. From the very summit of the house a little spout—the overflow, no doubt, of some unknown receptacle under the roof—lets fall a succession of drops that is almost a continuous stream. Down it falls, this all but stream, a sheer forty or fifty feet on to the stones of the basement steps, thence to dribble ignominiously away into some appointed drain. The cataracts blow their trumpets from the steep; but my lesser waterfalls play a subtler, I had almost said a more " modern " music. Lying awake at nights, I listen with a mixture of pleasure and irritation to its curious cadences.

The musical range of a dripping tap is about half an octave. But within the bounds of this major fourth, drops can play the most surprising and varied melodies. You will hear them climbing laboriously up small degrees of sound, only to descend at a single leap to the bottom. More often they wander unaccountably about in varying intervals, familiar or disconcertingly odd. And with the varying pitch the time also varies, but within narrower limits. For the laws of hydrostatics, or whatever other science claims authority over drops, do not allow the dribblings much licence either to pause or to quicken the pace of their falling. It is an odd sort of music. One listens to it as one lies in bed, slipping gradually into sleep, with a curious, uneasy emotion.

Drip drop, drip drap drep drop. So it goes on, this watery melody, for ever without an end. Inconclusive, inconsequent, formless, it is always on the point of deviating into sense and form. Every now and then you will hear a complete phrase of rounded melody. And then—drip drop, di-drep, di-drap—the old inconsequence sets in once more. But suppose there were some significance in it ! It is that which troubles my drowsy mind as I listen at night. Perhaps for those who have ears to hear, this endless dribbling is as pregnant with thought and emotion, as significant as a piece of Bach. Drip drop, di-drap, di-drep. So little would suffice to turn the incoherence into meaning. The music of the drops is the symbol and type of the whole universe ; it is for ever, as it were, asymptotic to sense, infinitely close to significance, but never touching it. Never, unless the human mind comes and pulls it forcibly over the dividing space. If I could understand this wandering music, if I could detect in it a sequence, if I could force it to some conclusion—the diapason closing full in God, in mind, I hardly care what, so long as it closes in something definite—then, I feel, I should understand the whole incomprehensible machine, from the gaps between the stars to the policy of the Allies. And growing drowsier and drowsier, I listen to the ceaseless tune, the hollow soliloquy in the cistern, the sharp metallic rapping of the drops that fall from the roof upon the stones below ; and surely I begin to discover a meaning, surely I detect a trace of thought, surely the phrases follow one another with art, leading on inevitably to some prodigious conclusion. Almost I have it, almost, almost. . . . Then, I suppose, I fall definitely to sleep. For the next thing I am aware of is that the sunlight is streaming in. It is morning, and the water is still dripping as irritatingly and persistently as ever.

Sometimes the incoherence of the drop music is too much to be borne. The listener insists that the asymptote shall somehow touch the line of sense. He forces the drops to say something. He demands of them that they shall play, shall we say, " God Save the King," or the Hymn to Joy from the Ninth Symphony, or *Voi che Sapete*. The drops obey reluctantly ; they play what you desire, but with more than the ineptitude of the child at the piano. Still they play it somehow. But this is an extremely dangerous method of laying the haunting ghost whose voice is the drip of water. For once you have given the drops something to sing or say, they will go on singing and saying it for ever. Sleep becomes impossible, and at the two or three hundredth repetition of *Madelon* or even of an air from *Figaro* the mind begins to totter towards insanity.

WATER MUSIC

Drops, ticking clocks, machinery, everything that throbs or clicks or hums or hammers, can be made, with a little perseverance, to say something. In my childhood, I remember, I was told that trains said, " To Lancashire, to Lancashire, to fetch a pocket handkercher "— and *da capo* ad infinitum. They can also repeat, if desired, that useful piece of information : " To stop the train, pull down the chain." But it is very hard to persuade them to add the menacing corollary : " Penalty for improper use, Five Pounds." Still, with careful tutoring I have succeeded in teaching a train to repeat even that unrhythmical phrase.

Dadaist literature always reminds me a little of my falling drops. Confronted by it, I feel the same uncomfortable emotion as is begotten in me by the inconsequent music of water. Suppose, after all, that this apparently accidental sequence of words should contain the secret of art and life and the universe ! It may ; who knows ? And here am I, left out in the cold of total incomprehension ; and I pore over this literature and regard it upside down in the hope of discovering that secret. But somehow I cannot induce the words to take on any meaning whatever. Drip drop, di-drap, di-drep—Tzara and Picabia let fall their words and I am baffled. But I can see that there are great possibilities in this type of literature. For the tired journalist it is ideal, since it is not he, but the reader who has to do all the work. All he need do is to lean back in his chair and allow the words to dribble out through the nozzle of his fountain pen. Drip, drop . . .

PLEASURES

WE have heard a great deal, since 1914, about the things which are a menace to civilization. First it was Prussian militarism ; then the Germans at large ; then the prolongation of the war ; then the shortening of the same ; then, after a time, the Treaty of Versailles ; then French militarism—with, all the while, a running accompaniment of such minor menaces as Prohibition, Lord Northcliffe, Mr. Bryan, Comstockery . . .

Civilization, however, has resisted the combined attacks of these enemies wonderfully well. For still, in 1923, it stands not so very far from where it stood in that " giant age before the flood " of nine years since. Where, in relation to Neanderthal on the one hand and Athens on the other, where precisely it stood *then* is a question which each may answer according to his taste. The important fact is that these menaces to our civilization, such as it is—menaces including the largest war and the stupidest peace known to history—have confined themselves in most places and up till now to mere threats, barking more furiously than they bite.

No, the dangers which confront our civilization are not so much the external dangers—wild men, wars and the bankruptcy that wars bring after them. The most alarming dangers are those which menace it from within, that threaten the mind rather than the body and estate of contemporary man.

Of all the various poisons which modern civilization, by a process of auto-intoxication, brews quietly up within its own bowels, few, it seems to me, are more deadly (while none appears more harmless) than that curious and appalling thing that is technically known as " pleasure." " Pleasure " (I place the word between inverted commas to show that I mean, not real pleasure, but the organized activities officially known by the same name) " pleasure "—what nightmare visions the word evokes ! Like every man of sense and good feeling, I abominate work. But I would rather put in eight hours a day at a Government office than be condemned to lead a life of " pleasure " ; I would even, I believe, prefer to write a million words of journalism a year.

The horrors of modern " pleasure "

arise from the fact that every kind of organized distraction tends to become progressively more and more imbecile. There was a time when people indulged themselves with distractions requiring the expense of a certain intellectual effort. In the seventeenth century, for example, royal personages and their courtiers took a real delight in listening to erudite sermons (Dr. Donne's, for example) and academical disputes on points of theology or metaphysics. Part of the entertainment offered to the Prince Palatine, on the occasion of his marriage with James I.'s daughter, was a syllogistic argumentation, on I forget what philosophical theme, between the amiable Lord Keeper Williams and a troop of minor Cambridge logicians. Imagine the feelings of a contemporary prince, if a loyal University were to offer him a similar entertainment!

Royal personages were not the only people who enjoyed intelligent pleasures. In Elizabethan times every lady and gentleman of ordinary culture could be relied upon, at demand, to take his or her part in a madrigal or a motet. Those who know the enormous complexity and subtlety of sixteenth-century music will realize what this means. To indulge in their favourite pastime our ancestors had to exert their minds to an uncommon degree. Even the uneducated vulgar delighted in pleasures requiring the exercise of a certain intelligence, individuality and personal initiative. They listened, for example, to *Othello*, *King Lear*, and *Hamlet*—apparently with enjoyment and comprehension. They sang and made much music. And far away, in the remote country, the peasants, year by year, went through the traditional rites—the dances of spring and summer, the winter mummings, the ceremonies of harvest home—appropriate to each successive season. Their pleasures were intelligent and alive, and it was they who, by their own efforts, entertained themselves.

We have changed all that. In place of the old pleasures demanding intelligence and personal initiative, we have vast organizations that provide us with ready-made distractions — distractions which demand from pleasure-seekers no personal participation and no intellectual effort of any sort. To the interminable democracies of the world a million cinemas bring the same stale balderdash. There have always been fourth-rate writers and dramatists ; but their works, in the past, quickly died without getting beyond the boundaries of the city or the country in which they appeared. To-day, the inventions of the scenario-writer go out from Los Angeles across the whole world. Countless audiences soak passively in the tepid bath of nonsense. No mental effort is demanded of them, no participation ; they need only sit and keep their eyes open.

Do the democracies want music ? In the old days they would have made it themselves. Now, they merely turn on the gramophone. Or if they are a little more up-to-date they adjust their wireless telephone to the right wave-length and listen-in to the fruity contralto at Marconi House, singing " The Gleaner's Slumber Song."

And if they want literature, there is the Press. Nominally, it is true, the Press exists to impart information. But its real function is to provide, like the cinema, a distraction which shall occupy the mind without demanding of it the slightest effort or the fatigue of a single thought. This function, it must be admitted, it fulfils with an extraordinary success. It is possible to go on for years and years, reading two papers every working day and one on Sundays without ever once being called upon to think or to make any other effort than to move the eyes, not very attentively, down the printed column.

Certain sections of the community still practise athletic sports in which individual participation is demanded. Great numbers of the middle and upper classes play golf and tennis in person and, if they are sufficiently rich, shoot birds and pursue the fox and go ski-ing in the Alps. But the vast mass of the community has now come even to sport vicariously, preferring the watching of football to the fatigues and dangers of the actual game. All classes, it is true, still dance ; but dance, all the world over, the same steps to the same tunes. The dance has been scrupulously steril-ized of any local or personal individuality.

These effortless pleasures, these ready-made distractions that are the same for every one over the face of the whole

PLEASURES

Western world, are surely a worse menace
to our civilization than ever the Germans
were. The working hours of the day
are already, for the great majority of
human beings, occupied in the performance of purely mechanical tasks in which
no mental effort, no individuality, no
initiative are required. And now, in
the hours of leisure, we turn to distractions as mechanically stereotyped and
demanding as little intelligence and
initiative as does our work. Add such
leisure to such work and the sum is a
perfect day which it is a blessed relief
to come to the end of.

Self-poisoned in this fashion, civilization looks as though it might easily decline
into a kind of premature senility. With a
mind almost atrophied by lack of use,
unable to entertain itself and grown so
wearily uninterested in the ready-made
distractions offered from without that
nothing but the grossest stimulants of an
ever-increasing violence and crudity can
move it, the democracy of the future
will sicken of a chronic and mortal boredom. It will go, perhaps, the way the
Romans went : the Romans who came
at last to lose, precisely as we are doing

now, the capacity to distract themselves ; the Romans who, like us, lived on ready-made entertainments in which they had no participation. Their deadly ennui demanded ever more gladiators, more tightrope-walking elephants, more rare and far-fetched animals to be slaughtered. Ours would demand no less ; but owing to the existence of a few idealists, doesn't get all it asks for. The most violent forms of entertainment can only be obtained illicitly ; to satisfy a taste for slaughter and cruelty you must become a member of the Klu Klux Klan. Let us not despair, however ; we may still live to see blood flowing across the stage of the Hippodrome. The force of a boredom clamouring to be alleviated may yet prove too much for the idealists.

MODERN FOLK POETRY

To all those who are interested in the " folk " and their poetry—the contemporary folk of the great cities and their urban muse—I would recommend a little-known journal called *McGlennon's Pantomime Annual*. This periodical makes its appearance at some time in the New Year, when the pantos are slowly withering away under the influence of approaching spring. I take this opportunity of warning my readers to keep a sharp look out for the coming of the next issue ; it is sure to be worth the modest twopence which one is asked to pay for it.

McGlennon's Pantomine Annual is an anthology of the lyrics of the panto season's most popular songs. It is a document of first-class importance. To the future student of our popular literature *McGlennon* will be as precious as the Christie-Miller collection of Elizabethan broadsheets. In the year 2220 a copy of the *Pantomime Annual* may very likely sell for hundreds of pounds at the Sotheby's of the time. With laudable forethought I am preserving my copy of last year's *McGlennon*

for the enrichment of my distant pos-
terity.

The Folk Poetry of 1920 may best
be classified according to subject-matter.
First, by reason of its tender associations
as well as its mere amount, is the poetry
of Passion. Then there is the Poetry
of Filial Devotion. Next, the Poetry of
the Home—the dear old earthly Home
in Oregon or Kentucky—and, complementary to it, the Poetry of the Spiritual
Home in other and happier worlds.
Here, as well as in the next section, the
popular lyric borrows some of its best
effects from hymnology. There follows
the Poetry of Recollection and Regret,
and the Poetry of Nationality, a type
devoted almost exclusively to the praises
of Ireland. These types and their variations cover the Folk's serious poetry.
Their comic vein is less susceptible to
analysis. Drink, Wives, Young Nuts,
Honeymoon Couples—these are a few of
the stock subjects.

The Amorous Poetry of the Folk, like
the love lyrics of more cultured poets,
is divided into two species : the Poetry
of Spiritual Amour and the more direct
and concrete expression of Immediate

MODERN FOLK POETRY

Desire. *McGlennon* provides plenty of examples of both types :

When love peeps in the window of your heart

[it might be the first line of a Shakespeare sonnet]

> You seem to walk on air,
> Birds sing their sweet songs to you,
> No cloud in your skies of blue,
> Sunshine all the happy day, etc.

These rhapsodies tend to become a little tedious. But one feels the warm touch of reality in

> I want to snuggle, I want to snuggle,
> I know a cosy place for two.
> I want to snuggle, I want to snuggle,
> I want to feel that love is true.
> Take me in your arms as lovers do.
> Hold me very tight and kiss me too.
> I want to snuggle, I want to snuggle,
> I want to snuggle close to you.

This is sound ; but it does not come up to the best of the popular lyrics. The agonized passion expressed in the words and music of " You Made Me Love You " is something one does not easily forget, though that great song is as old as the now distant origins of ragtime.

ON THE MARGIN

The Poetry of Filial Devotion is almost as extensive as the Poetry of Amour. *McGlennon* teems with such outbursts as this :

You are a wonderful mother, dear old mother
    of mine.
You'll hold a spot down deep in my heart
Till the stars no longer shine.
Your soul shall live on for ever,
On through the fields of time,
For there'll never be another to me
Like that wonderful mother of mine.

Even Grandmamma gets a share of this devotion :

Granny, my own, I seem to hear you calling
    me ;
Granny, my own, you are my sweetest
    memory . . .
If up in heaven angels reign supreme,
Among the angels you must be the Queen.
Granny, my own, I miss you more and more.

The last lines are particularly rich. What a fascinating heresy, to hold that the angels reign over their Creator !

The Poetry of Recollection and Regret owes most, both in words and music, to the hymn. *McGlennon* provides a

56

choice example in " Back from the Land of Yesterday " :

> Back from the land of yesterday,
>   Back to the friends of yore ;
> Back through the dark and dreary way
>   Into the light once more.
> Back to the heart that waits for me,
>   Warmed by the sunshine above ;
> Back from the old land of yesterday's dreams
>   To a new land of life and love.

What it means, goodness only knows. But one can imagine that, sung to a slow music in three-four time — some rich religious waltz-tune—it would be extremely uplifting and edifying. The decay of regular churchgoing has inevitably led to this invasion of the music-hall by the hymn. People still want to feel the good uplifting emotion, and they feel it with a vengeance when they listen to songs about

> the land of beginning again,
> Where skies are always blue . . .
> Where broken dreams come true.

The great advantage of the music-hall over the church is that the uplifting moments do not last too long.

Finally, there is the great Home motif. " I want to be," these lyrics always begin, " I want to be almost anywhere that is not the place where I happen at the moment to be." M. Louis Estève has called this longing " Le Mal de la Province," which in its turn is closely related to " Le Mal de l'au-delà." It is one of the worst symptoms of romanticism.

> Steamer, balançant ta mâture,
> Lève l'ancre vers une exotique nature,

exclaims Mallarmé, and the Folk, whom that most exquisite of poets loathed and despised, echo his words in a hundred different keys. There is not a State in America where they don't want to go. In *McGlennon* we find yearnings expressed for California, Ohio, Tennessee, Virginia, and Georgia. Some sigh for Ireland, Devon, and the East. " Egypt ! I am calling you ; Oh, life is sweet and joys complete when at your feet I lay [*sic*]." But the Southern States, the East, Devon, and Killarney are not enough. The Mal de l'au-delà succeeds the Mal de la Province. The Folk yearn for extra-mundane worlds. Here, for example, is

MODERN FOLK POETRY

an expression of nostalgia for a mystical
" Kingdom within your Eyes " :

> Somewhere in somebody's eyes
>   Is a place just divine,
> Bounded by roses that kiss the dew
>   In those dear eyes that shine.
> Somewhere beyond earthly dreams,
>   Where love's flower never dies,
> God made the world, and He gave it to me
>   In that kingdom within your eyes.

If there is any characteristic which distinguishes contemporary folk poetry from
the folk poetry of other times it is surely
its meaninglessness. Old folk poetry
is singularly direct and to the point,
full of pregnant meaning, never vague.
Modern folk poetry, as exemplified in
McGlennon, is almost perfectly senseless.
The Elizabethan peasant or mechanic
would never have consented to sing or
listen to anything so flatulently meaningless as " Back from the Land of Yesterday " or " The Kingdom within your
Eyes." His taste was for something clear,
definite and pregnant, like "Greensleeves":

> And every morning when you rose,
>   I brought you dainties orderly,
> To clear your stomach from all woes—
>   And yet you would not love me.

Could anything be more logical and to the point ?   But we, instead of logic, instead of clarity, are provided by our professional entertainers with the drivelling imbecility of " Granny, my own." Can it be that the standard of intelligence is lower now than it was three hundred years ago ?   Have newspapers and cinemas and now the wireless telephone conspired to rob mankind of whatever sense of reality, whatever power of individual questioning and criticism he once possessed ?   I do not venture to answer. But the fact of *McGlennon* has somehow got to be explained.   How ?   I prefer to leave the problem on a note of interrogation.

BIBLIOPHILY

BIBLIOPHILY is on the increase. It is a constatation which I make with regret; for the bibliophile's point of view is, to me at least, unsympathetic and his standard of values unsound. Among the French, bibliophily would seem to have become a kind of mania, and, what is more, a highly organized and thoroughly exploited mania. Whenever I get a new French book I turn at once—for in what disgusts and irritates one there is always a certain odious fascination—to the fly-leaf. One had always been accustomed to finding there a brief description of the " vingt exemplaires sur papier hollande Van Gelder "; nobody objected to the modest old Dutchman whose paper gave to the author's presentation copies so handsome an appearance. But Van Gelder is now a back number. In this third decade of the twentieth century he has become altogether too simple and unsophisticated. On the fly-leaf of a *dernière nouveauté* I find the following incantation, printed in block capitals and occupying at least twenty lines :

Il a été tiré de cet ouvrage, après imposi-

61

tions spéciales, 133 exemplaires in-4. Tellière sur papier-vergé pur-fil Lafuma-Navarre, au filigrane de la *Nouvelle Revue Française*, dont 18 exemplaires hors commerce, marqués de A à R, 100 exemplaires réservés aux Bibliophiles de la *Nouvelle Revue Française*, numérotés de I à C, 15 exemplaires numérotés de CI à CXV ; 1040 exemplaires sur papier vélin pur-fil Lafuma-Navarre, dont dix exemplaires hors commerce marqués de a à j, 800 exemplaires réservés aux amis de l'Edition originale, numérotes de 1 à 800, 30 exemplaires d'auteur, hors commerce, numérotés de 801 à 830 et 200 exemplaires numérotés de 831 à 1030, ce tirage constituant proprement et authentiquement l'Edition originale.

If I were one of the hundred Biblio-philes of the *Nouvelle Revue Française* or even one of the eight hundred Friends of the Original Edition, I should suggest, with the utmost politeness, that the publishers might deserve better of their fellow-beings if they spent less pains on numbering the first edition and more on seeing that it was properly produced. Personally, I am the friend of any edition which is reasonably well printed and bound, reasonably correct in the text and reasonably clean. The conscious-ness that I possess a numbered copy of an edition printed on Lafuma-Navarre paper, duly watermarked with the publisher's initials, does not make up for the fact that the book is full of gross printer's errors and that a whole sheet of sixteen pages has wandered, during the process of binding, from one end of the volume to the other—occurrences which are quite unnecessarily frequent in the history of French book production.

With the increased attention paid to bibliophilous niceties, has come a great increase in price. Limited *éditions de luxe* have become absurdly common in France, and there are dozens of small publishing concerns which produce almost nothing else. Authors like Monsieur André Salmon and Monsieur Max Jacob scarcely ever appear at less than twenty francs a volume. Even with the exchange this is a formidable price ; and yet the French bibliophiles, for whom twenty francs are really twenty francs, appear to have an insatiable appetite for these small and beautiful editions. The War has established a new economic law : the poorer one becomes the more one can afford to spend on luxuries.

The ordinary English publisher has

never gone in for Van Gelder, Lafuma-Navarre and numbered editions. Reticent about figures, he leaves the book collector to estimate the first edition's future rarity by guess-work. He creates no artificial scarcity values. The collector of contemporary English first editions is wholly a speculator ; he never knows what time may have in store.

In the picture trade for years past nobody has pretended that there was any particular relation between the price of a picture and its value as a work of art. A magnificent El Greco is bought for about a tenth of the sum paid for a Romney that would be condemned by any self-respecting hanging-committee. We are so well used to this sort of thing in picture dealing that we have almost ceased to comment on it. But in the book trade the tendency to create huge artificial values is of a later growth. The spectacle of a single book being bought for fifteen thousand pounds is still sufficiently novel to arouse indignation. Moreover, the book collector who pays vast sums for his treasures has even less excuse than has the collector of pictures. The value of an old book is wholly a scarcity value. From a picture one may get a genuine æsthetic pleasure; in buying a picture one buys the unique right to feel that pleasure. But nobody can pretend that *Venus and Adonis* is more delightful when it is read in a fifteen thousand pound unique copy than when it is read in a volume that has cost a shilling. On the whole, the printing and general appearance of the shilling book is likely to be the better of the two. The purchaser of the fabulously expensive old book is satisfying only his possessive instinct. The buyer of a picture may also have a genuine feeling for beauty.

The triumph and the *reductio ad absurdum* of bibliophily were witnessed not long ago at Sotheby's, when the late Mr. Smith of New York bought eighty thousand pounds' worth of books in something under two hours at the Britwell Court sale. The War, it is said, created forty thousand new millionaires in America; the New York bookseller can have had no lack of potential clients. He bought a thousand-guinea volume as an ordinary human being might buy something off the sixpenny shelf in a second-hand shop. I have seldom witnessed a spectacle which inspired in me an intenser blast of moral indignation. Moral indignation, of course, is always to be mistrusted as, wholly or in part, the disguised manifestation of some ignoble passion. In this case the basic cause of my indignation was clearly envy. But there was, I flatter myself, a superstructure of disinterested moral feeling. To debase a book into an expensive object of luxury is as surely, in Miltonic language, " to kill the image of God, as it were in the eye," as to burn it. And when one thinks how those eighty thousand pounds might have been spent. . . . Ah, well !

DEMOCRATIC ART

THERE is intoxication to be found in a crowd. For it is good to be one of many all doing the same thing— good whatever the thing may be, whether singing hymns, watching a football match, or applauding the eternal truths of politicians. Anything will serve as an excuse. It matters not in whose name your two or three thousand are gathered together ; what is important is the process of gathering. In these last days we have witnessed a most illuminating example of this tendency in the wild outburst of mob excitement over the arrival in this country of Mary Pickford. It is not as though people were really very much interested in the Little Sweetheart of the World. She is no more than an excuse for assembling in a crowd and working up a powerful communal emotion. The newspapers set the excitement going ; they built the fire, applied the match, and cherished the infant flame. The crowds, only too happy to be kindled, did the rest ; they burned.

I belong to that class of unhappy people who are not easily infected by crowd excitement. Too often I find myself

sadly and coldly unmoved in the midst
of multitudinous emotion. Few sensations are more disagreeable. The defect
is in part temperamental, and in part
is due to that intellectual snobbishness,
that fastidious rejection of what is easy
and obvious, which is one of the melancholy consequences of the acquisition of
culture. How often one regrets this
asceticism of the mind ! How wistfully
sometimes one longs to be able to rid
oneself of the habit of rejection and
selection, and to enjoy all the dear,
obviously luscious, idiotic emotions without an afterthought ! And indeed, however much we may admire the Chromatic
Fantasia of Bach, we all of us have a soft
spot somewhere in our minds that is
sensitive to " Roses in Picardy." But the
soft spot is surrounded by hard spots ;
the enjoyment is never unmixed with
critical disapprobation. The excuses for
working up a communal emotion, even
communal emotion itself, are rejected
as too gross. We turn from them as a
cœnobite of the Thebaid would have
turned from dancing girls or a steaming
dish of tripe and onions.

I have before me now a little book,

recently arrived from America, which points out the way in which the random mob emotion may be systematically organized into a kind of religion. This volume, *The Will of Song* (Boni & Liveright, 70 c.), is the joint production of Messrs. Harry Barnhart and Percy MacKaye. "How are art and social service to be reconciled ? . . . How shall the Hermit Soul of the Individual Poet give valid, spontaneous expression to the Communal Soul of assembled multitudes ? How may the surging Tides of Man be sluiced in Conduits of Art, without losing their primal glory and momentum ? " These questions and many others, involving a great expense of capital letters, are asked by Mr. MacKaye and answered in *The Will of Song*, which bears the qualifying subtitle, "A Dramatic Service of Community Singing."

The service is democratically undogmatic. Abstractions, such as Will, Imagination, Joy, Love and Liberty, some of whom are represented in the dramatic performance, not by individuals, but by Group Personages (*i.e.* choruses), chant about Brotherhood in a semi-Biblical phraseology that is almost wholly empty of content. It is all delightfully vague and non-committal, like a Cabinet Minister's speech about the League of Nations, and, like such a speech, leaves behind it a comfortable glow, a noble feeling of uplift. But, like Cabinet Ministers, preachers and all whose profession it is to move the people by the emission of words, the authors of *The Will of Song* are well aware that what matters in a popular work of art is not the intellectual content so much as the picturesqueness of its form and the emotion with which it is presented. In the staging—if such a term is not irreverent—of their service, Messrs. Barnhart and MacKaye have borrowed from Roman Catholic ritual all its most effective emotion-creators. The darknesses, the illuminations, the chiming bells, the solemn mysterious voices, the choral responses—all these traditional devices have been most scientifically exploited in the Communal Service.

These are the stage directions which herald the opening of the service :

As the final song of the Prelude ceases, the assembly hall grows suddenly dark, and the

DEMOCRATIC ART

DARKNESS is filled with fanfare of blowing
TRUMPETS. And now, taking up the trumpets'
refrain, the Orchestra plays an elemental music,
suggestive of rain, wind, thunder and the
rushing of waters; from behind the raised
Central Seat great Flashes of Fire spout up-
ward, and while they are flaring there rises a
FLAME GOLD FIGURE, in a cone of light, who
calls with deep, vibrant voice : " Who has risen
up from the heart of the people ? " Instantan-
eous, from three portions of the assembly, the
VOICES OF THREE GROUPS, Men, Women and
Children, answer from the dark in triple unison :
" I ! "

Even from the cold print one can see
that this opening would be extremely
effective. But doubts assail me. I have
a horrid suspicion that that elemental
music would not sweep me off my feet
as it ought to. My fears are justified
when, looking up the musical programme,
I discover that the elemental music is
by Langey, and that the orchestral accom-
paniments that follow are the work of
Massenet, Tschaikovsky, Langey once
more, Julia Ward Howe and Sinding.
Alas! once more one finds oneself the
slave of one's habit of selection and rejection. One would find oneself left out
in the cold just because one couldn't

71

stand Massenet. Those who have seen Sir James Barrie's latest play, *Mary Rose*, will perhaps recall the blasts of music which prelude the piece and recur at every mystical moment throughout the play. In theory one ought to have mounted on the wings of that music into a serene acceptance of Sir James Barrie's supernatural machinery; one ought to have been filled by it with deeply religious emotions. In practice, however, one found oneself shrinking with quivering nerves from the poignant vulgarity of that *Leitmotif*, isolated by what should have united one with the author and the rest of the audience. The cœnobite would like to eat the tripe and onions, but finds by experiment that the smell of the dish makes him feel rather sick.

One must not, however, reject such things as *The Will of Song* as absolutely and entirely bad. They are useful, they are even good, on their own plane and for people who belong to a certain order of the spiritual hierarchy. *The Will of Song*, set to elemental music by Massenet and Julia Ward Howe, may be a moving spiritual force for people to whom, shall we say, Wagner means nothing; just as Wagner himself may be of spiritual importance to people belonging to a slightly higher caste, but still incapable of understanding or getting any good out of the highest, the transcendent works of art—out of the Mass in D, for example, or Sonata Op. 111.

The democratically minded will ask what right we have to say that the Mass in D is better than the works of Julia Ward Howe, what right we have to assign a lower place in the spiritual hierarchy to the admirers of *The Will of Song* than to the admirers of Beethoven. They will insist that there is no hierarchy at all; that every creature possessing humanity, possessing even life, is as good and as important, by the mere fact of that possession, as any other creature. It is not altogether easy to answer these objections. The arguments on both sides are ultimately based on conviction and faith. The best one can do to convince the paradoxical democrat of the real superiority of the Mass in D over the *Will of Song* is to point out that, in a sense, one contains the other; that *The Will of Song* is a part, and a very small part at that, of a great

Whole of human experience, to which the Mass in D much more nearly approximates. In *The Will of Song* and its " elemental " accompaniment one knows exactly how every effect is obtained ; its range of emotional and intellectual experience is extremely limited and perfectly familiar. But the range of the Mass in D is enormously much larger ; it includes within itself the range of *The Will of Song*, takes it for granted, so to speak, and reaches out into remoter spheres of experience. It is in a real sense quantitatively larger than *The Will of Song*. To the democrat who believes in majorities this is an argument which must surely prove convincing.

ACCUMULATIONS

IN the brevity of life and the perishableness of material things the moral philosophers have always found one of their happiest themes. " Time, which antiquates Antiquities, hath an Art to make dust of all things." There is nothing more moving than those swelling elegiac organ notes in which they have celebrated the mortality of man and all his works. Those of us for whom the proper study of mankind is books dwell with the most poignant melancholy over the destruction of literary treasures. We think of all the pre-Platonic philosophers of whose writings only a few sentences remain. We think of Sappho's poems, all but completely blotted from our knowledge. We think of the missing fragments of the " Satyricon," and of many other precious pages which once were and are now no more. We complain of the holes that time has picked in the records of history, bewailing the loss of innumerable vanished documents. As for buildings, pictures, statues and the accumulated evidence of whole civilizations, all destroyed as though they had never been, they do not belong to our literary province, and, if they did, would be too numerous to catalogue even summarily.

But because men have once thought and felt in a certain way it does not follow that they will for ever continue to do so. There seems every probability that our descendants, some two or three centuries hence, will wax pathetic in their complaints, not of the fragility, but the horrible persistence and indestructibility of things. They will feel themselves smothered by the intolerable accumulation of the years. The men of to-day are so deeply penetrated with the sense of the perishableness of matter that they have begun to take immense precautions to preserve everything they can. Desolated by the carelessness of our ancestors, we are making very sure that our descendants shall lack no documents when they come to write our history. All is systematically kept and catalogued. Old things are carefully patched and propped into continued existence ; things now new are hoarded up and protected from decay.

To walk through the book-stores of one of the world's great libraries is an experi-

ence that cannot fail to set one thinking on the appalling indestructibility of
matter. A few years ago I explored
the recently dug cellars into which the
overflow of the Bodleian pours in an
unceasing stream. The cellars extend
under the northern half of the great
quadrangle in whose centre stands the
Radcliffe Camera. These catacombs are
two storeys deep and lined with imper-
meable concrete. " The muddy damps
and ropy slime " of the traditional vault
are absent in this great necropolis of
letters ; huge ventilating pipes breathe
blasts of a dry and heated wind, that
makes the place as snug and as unsympathetic to decay as the deserts of Central
Asia. The books stand in metal cases
constructed so as to slide in and out of
position on rails. So ingenious is the
arrangement of the cases that it is possible
to fill two-thirds of the available space,
solidly, with books. Twenty years or
so hence, when the existing vaults will
take no more books, a new cellar can be
dug on the opposite side of the Camera.
And when that is full—it is only a matter
of half a century from now—what then ?
We shrug our shoulders. After us the

deluge. But let us hope that Bodley's Librarian of 1970 will have the courage to emend the last word to " bonfire." To the bonfire ! That is the only satisfactory solution of an intolerable problem.

The deliberate preservation of things must be compensated for by their deliberate and judicious destruction. Otherwise the world will be overwhelmed by the accumulation of antique objects. Pigs and rabbits and watercress, when they were first introduced into New Zealand, threatened to lay waste the country, because there were no compensating forces of destruction to put a stop to their indefinite multiplication. In the same way, mere things, once they are set above the natural laws of decay, will end by burying us, unless we set about methodically to get rid of the nuisance. The plea that they should all be preserved—every novel by Nat Gould, every issue of the *Funny Wonder*— as historical documents is not a sound one. Where too many documents exist it is impossible to write history at all. " For ignorance," in the felicitous words of Mr. Lytton Strachey, " is the first requisite of the historian — ignorance which simplifies and clarifies, which selects and omits, with a placid perfection unattainable by the highest art." Nobody wants to know everything—the irrelevancies as well as the important facts—about the past; or in any case nobody ought to desire to know. Those who do, those who are eaten up by an itch for mere facts and useless information, are the wretched victims of a vice no less reprehensible than greed or drunkenness.

Hand in hand with this judicious process of destruction must go an elaborate classification of what remains. As Mr. Wells says in his large, opulent way, " the future world-state's organization of scientific research and record compared with that of to-day will be like an ocean liner beside the dug-out canoe of some early heliolithic wanderer." With the vast and indiscriminate multiplication of books and periodicals our organization of records tends to become ever more heliolithic. Useful information on any given subject is so widely scattered or may be hidden in such obscure places that the student is often at a loss to know what he ought to study or where. An immense international labour of bibliography and classification must be undertaken at no very distant date, if future generations of researchers are to make the fullest use of the knowledge that has already been gained.

But this constructive labour will be tedious and insipid compared with the glorious business of destruction. Huge bonfires of paper will blaze for days and weeks together, whenever the libraries undertake their periodical purgation. The only danger, and, alas! it is a very real danger, is that the libraries will infallibly purge themselves of the wrong books. We all know what librarians are; and not only librarians, but critics, literary men, general public—everybody, in fact, with the exception of ourselves— we know what they are like, we know them: there never was a set of people with such bad taste! Committees will doubtless be set up to pass judgment on books, awarding acquittals and condemnations in magisterial fashion. It will be a sort of gigantic Hawthornden competition. At that thought I find that the flames of my great bonfires lose much of their imagined lustre.

ON DEVIATING INTO SENSE

THERE is a story, very dear for some reason to our ancestors, that Apelles, or I forget what other Greek painter, grown desperate at the failure of his efforts to portray realistically the foam on a dog's mouth, threw his sponge at the picture in a pet, and was rewarded for his ill-temper by discovering that the resultant smudge was the living image of the froth whose aspect he had been unable, with all his art, to recapture. No one will ever know the history of all the happy mistakes, the accidents and unconscious deviations into genius, that have helped to enrich the world's art. They are probably countless. I myself have deviated more than once into accidental felicities. Recently, for example, the hazards of careless typewriting caused me to invent a new portmanteau word of the most brilliantly Laforguian quality. I had meant to write the phrase " the Human Comedy," but, by a happy slip, I put my finger on the letter that stands next to " C " on the universal keyboard. When I came to read over the completed page I found that I had written " the Human Vomedy."

Was there ever a criticism of life more succinct and expressive ? To the more sensitive and queasy among the gods the last few years must indeed have seemed a vomedy of the first order.

The grossest forms of mistake have played quite a distinguished part in the history of letters. One thinks, for example, of the name Criseida or Cressida manufactured out of a Greek accusative, of that Spenserian misunderstanding of Chaucer which gave currency to the rather ridiculous substantive " derring-do." Less familiar, but more deliciously absurd, is Chaucer's slip in reading " naves ballatrices " for " naves bellatrices "— ballet-ships instead of battle-ships—and his translation " shippes hoppesteres." But these broad, straightforward howlers are uninteresting compared with the more subtle deviations into originality occasionally achieved by authors who were trying their best not to be original. Nowhere do we find more remarkable examples of accidental brilliance than among the post-Chaucerian poets, whose very indistinct knowledge of what precisely *was* the metre in which they were trying to write often caused them to produce very striking variations on the staple English measure.

Chaucer's variations from the decasyllable norm were deliberate. So, for the most part, were those of his disciple Lydgate, whose favourite " broken-backed " line, lacking the first syllable of the iambus that follows the cæsura, is metrically of the greatest interest to contemporary poets. Lydgate's characteristic line follows this model :

For speechéless nothing maist thou speed.

Judiciously employed, the broken-backed line might yield very beautiful effects. Lydgate, as has been said, was probably pretty conscious of what he was doing. But his procrustean methods were apt to be a little indiscriminate, and one wonders sometimes whether he was playing variations on a known theme or whether he was rather tentatively groping after the beautiful regularity of his master Chaucer. The later fifteenth and sixteenth century poets seem to have worked very much in the dark. The poems of such writers as Hawes and Skelton abound in the vaguest parodies of the decasyllable line. Anything from seven to fifteen syllables

83

will serve their turn. With them the variations are seldom interesting. Chance had not much opportunity of producing subtle metrical effects with a man like Skelton, whose mind was naturally so full of jigging doggerel that his variations on the decasyllable are mostly in the nature of rough skeltonics. I have found interesting accidental variations on the decasyllable in Heywood, the writer of moralities. This, from the *Play of Love*, has a real metrical beauty:

Felt ye but one pang such as I feel many,
One pang of despair or one pang of desire,
One pang of one displeasant look of her eye,
One pang of one word of her mouth as in ire,
Or in restraint of her love which I desire—
One pang of all these, felt once in all your life,
Should quail your opinion and quench all our
    strife.

These dactylic resolutions of the third and fourth lines are extremely interesting.

But the most remarkable example of accidental metrical invention that I have yet come across is to be found in the Earl of Surrey's translation of Horace's ode on the golden mean. Surrey was one of the pioneers of the reaction against the vagueness and uncertain care-

lessness of the post-Chaucerians. From the
example of Italian poetry he had learned
that a line must have a fixed number of
syllables. In all his poems his aim is always
to achieve regularity at whatever cost. To
make sure of having ten syllables in every
line it is evident that Surrey made use of
his fingers as well as his ears. We see him
at his worst and most laborious in the first
stanza of his translation :

Of thy life, Thomas, this compass well mark :
Not aye with full sails the high seas to beat ;
Ne by coward dread in shunning storms dark
On shallow shores thy keel in peril freat.

The ten syllables are there all right,
but except in the last line there is no
recognizable rhythm of any kind, whether
regular or irregular. But when Surrey
comes to the second stanza—

> Auream quisquis mediocritatem
> Diligit, tutus caret obsoleti
> Sordibus tecti, caret invidenda
> Sobrius aula—

some lucky accident inspires him with the
genius to translate in these words :

Whoso gladly halseth the golden mean,
Void of dangers advisedly hath his home ;
Not with loathsome muck as a den unclean,
Nor palace like, whereat disdain may gloam.

Not only is this a very good translation, but it is also a very interesting and subtle metrical experiment. What could be more felicitous than this stanza made up of three trochaic lines, quickened by beautiful dactylic resolutions, and a final iambic line of regular measure—the recognized tonic chord that brings the music to its close ? And yet the tunelessness of the first stanza is enough to prove that Surrey's achievement is as much a product of accident as the foam on the jaws of Apelles' dog. He was doing his best all the time to write decasyllables with the normal iambic beat of the last line. His failures to do so were sometimes unconscious strokes of genius.

POLITE CONVERSATION

THERE are some people to whom the most difficult to obey of all the commandments is that which enjoins us to suffer fools gladly. The prevalence of folly, its monumental, unchanging permanence and its almost invariable triumph over intelligence are phenomena which they cannot contemplate without experiencing a passion of righteous indignation or, at the least, of ill-temper. Sages like Anatole France, who can probe and anatomize human stupidity and still remain serenely detached, are rare. These reflections were suggested by a book recently published in New York and entitled *The American Credo*. The authors of this work are those *enfants terribles* of American criticism, Messrs. H. L. Mencken and George Jean Nathan. They have compiled a list of four hundred and eighty-eight articles of faith which form the fundamental Credo of the American people, prefacing them with a very entertaining essay on the national mind :

Truth shifts and changes like a cataract of diamonds ; its aspect is never precisely the same at two successive moments. But error

flows down the channel of history like some great
stream of lava or infinitely lethargic glacier.
It is the one relatively fixed thing in a world
of chaos.

To look through the articles of the Credo
is to realize that there is a good deal of
truth in this statement.   Such beliefs
as the following—not by any means
confined to America alone—are probably
at least as old as the Great Pyramid :

That if a woman, about to become a
mother, plays the piano every day, her
baby will be born a Victor Herbert.

That the accumulation of great wealth
always brings with it great unhappiness.

That it is bad luck to kill a spider.

That water rots the hair and thus
causes baldness.

That if a bride wears an old garter
with her new finery, she will have a happy
married life.

That children were much better be-
haved twenty years ago than they are
to-day.

And most of the others in the collection,
albeit clothed in forms distinctively contemporary and American, are simply
variations on notions as immemorial.

Inevitably, as one reads *The American*

POLITE CONVERSATION

Credo, one is reminded of an abler, a more pitiless and ferocious onslaught on stupidity, I mean Swift's " *Complete Collection of Genteel and Ingenious Conversation, according to the most polite mode and method now used at Court and in the Best Companies of England.* In three Dialogues. By Simon Wagstaff, Esq." I was inspired after reading Messrs. Mencken and Nathan's work to refresh my memories of this diabolic picture of the social amenities. And what a book it is ! There is something almost appalling in the way it goes on and on, a continuous, never-ceasing stream of imbecility. Simon Wagstaff, it will be remembered, spent the best part of forty years in collecting and digesting these gems of polite conversation :

I can faithfully assure the reader that there is not one single witty phrase in the whole Collection which has not received the Stamp and Approbation of at least One Hundred Years, and how much longer it is hard to determine ; he may therefore be secure to find them all genuine, sterling and authentic.

How genuine, sterling and authentic Mr. Wagstaff's treasures of polite conversation are is proved by the great

number of them which have withstood
all the ravages of time, and still do as
good service to-day as they did in the
early seventeen-hundreds or in the days
of Henry VIII. : " Go, you Girl, and
warm some fresh Cream." " Indeed,
Madam, there's none left ; for the Cat
has eaten it all." " I doubt it was a
Cat with Two Legs."

" And, pray, What News, Mr. Neverout ? " " Why, Madam, Queen Elizabeth's dead." (It would be interesting
to discover at exactly what date Queen
Anne took the place of Queen Elizabeth
in this grand old repartee, or who was
the monarch referred to when the Virgin
Queen was still alive. Aspirants to the
degree of B. or D.Litt. might do worse
than to take this problem as a subject
for their thesis.)

Some of the choicest phrases have come
down in the world since Mr. Wagstaff's
day. Thus, Miss Notable's retort to
Mr. Neverout, " Go, teach your Grannam
to suck Eggs," could only be heard now
in the dormitory of a preparatory school.
Others have become slightly modified.
Mr. Neverout says, " Well, all Things
have an End, and a pudden has two."

POLITE CONVERSATION

I think we may flatter ourselves that the modern emendation, "except a roly-poly pudding, which has two," is an improvement.

Mr. Wagstaff's second dialogue, wherein he treats of Polite Conversation at meals, contains more phrases that testify to the unbroken continuity of tradition than either of the others. The conversation that centres on the sirloin of beef is worthy to be recorded in its entirety:

LADY SMART. Come, Colonel, handle your Arms. Shall I help you to some Beef?

COLONEL. If your Ladyship please; and, pray, don't cut like a Mother-in-law, but send me a large Slice; for I love to lay a good Foundation. I vow, 'tis a noble Sir-loyn.

NEVEROUT. Ay; here's cut and come again.

MISS. But, pray; why is it call'd a Sir-loyn?

LORD SMART. Why, you must know that our King James the First, who lov'd good Eating, being invited to Dinner by one of his Nobles, and seeing a large Loyn of Beef at his Table, he drew out his Sword, and, in a Frolic, knighted it. Few people know the Secret of this.

How delightful it is to find that we have Mr. Wagstaff's warrant for such gems of wisdom as, "Cheese digests everything except itself," and "If you eat till you're cold, you'll live to grow old " ! If they were a hundred years old in his day they are fully three hundred now. Long may they survive! I was sorry, however, to notice that one of the best of Mr. Wagstaff's phrases has been, in the revolution of time, completely lost. Indeed, before I had read Aubrey's "Lives," Lord Sparkish's remark, "Come, box it about; 'twill come to my Father at last," was quite incomprehensible to me. The phrase is taken from a story of Sir Walter Raleigh and his son.

Sir Walter Raleigh [says Aubrey] being invited to dinner to some great person where his son was to goe with him, he sayd to his son, "Thou art expected to-day at dinner to goe along with me, but thou art so quarrelsome and affronting that I am ashamed to have such a beare in my company." Mr. Walter humbled himselfe to his father and promised he would behave himselfe mighty mannerly. So away they went. He sate next to his father and was very demure at least halfe dinner time. Then sayd he, "I this morning, not having the feare of God before my eies, butby the instigation of the devill, went . . ."

At this point Mr. Clark, in his edition, suppresses four lines of Aubrey's text;

but one can imagine the sort of thing
Master Walter said.

Sir Walter, being strangely surprized and putt
out of countenance at so great a table, gives
his son a damned blow over the face. His son,
as rude as he was, would not strike his father,
but strikes over the face the gentleman that
sate next to him and sayd, "Box about : 'twill
come to my father anon." 'Tis now a common-
used proverb.

And so it still deserves to be ; how, when
and why it became extinct, I have no idea.
Here is another good subject for a thesis.
There are but few things in Mr. Wagstaff's dialogue which appear definitely
out of date and strange to us, and these
superannuations can easily be accounted
for. Thus the repeal of the Criminal
Laws has made almost incomprehensible
the constant references to hanging made
by Mr. Wagstaff's personages. The oaths
and the occasional mild grossnesses have
gone out of fashion in mixed polite
society. Otherwise their conversation is
in all essentials exactly the same as the
conversation of the present day. And
this is not to be wondered at ; for, as a
wise man has said :

Speech at the present time retains strong

evidence of the survival in it of the function of herd recognition. . . . The function of conversation is ordinarily regarded as being the exchange of ideas and information. Doubtless it has come to have such a function, but an objective examination of ordinary conversation shows that the actual conveyance of ideas takes a very small part in it. As a rule the exchange seems to consist of ideas which are necessarily common to the two speakers and are known to be so by each. . . . Conversation between persons unknown to one another is apt to be rich in the ritual of recognition. When one hears or takes part in these elaborate evolutions, gingerly proffering one after another of one's marks of identity, one's views on the weather, on fresh air and draughts, on the Government and on uric acid, watching intently for the first low hint of a growl, which will show one belongs to the wrong pack and must withdraw, it is impossible not to be reminded of the similar manœuvres of the dog and to be thankful that Nature has provided us with a less direct, though perhaps a more tedious, code.

NATIONALITY IN LOVE

THE hazards of indiscriminate rummaging in bookshops have introduced me to two volumes of verse which seem to me (though I am ordinarily very sceptical of those grandiose generalizations about racial and national characteristics, so beloved of a certain class of literary people) to illustrate very clearly some of the differences between the French and English mind. The first is a little book published some few months back and entitled *Les Baisers*. . . . The publisher says of it in one of those exquisitely literary puffs which are the glory of the Paris book trade : " Un volume de vers ? Non pas ! Simplement des baisers mis en vers, des baisers variés comme l'heure qui passe, inconstants comme l'Amour lui-même. . . . Baisers, baisers, c'est toute leur troublante musique qui chante dans ces rimes." The other volume hails from the antipodes and is called *Songs of Love and Life*. No publisher's puff accompanies it ; but a coloured picture on the dustwrapper represents a nymph frantically clutching at a coy shepherd. A portrait of the authoress serves as a frontispiece.

Both books are erotic in character, and both are very indifferent in poetical quality. They are only interesting as illustrations, the more vivid because of their very second-rateness, of the two characteristic methods of approach, French and English, to the theme of physical passion.

The author of *Les Baisers* approaches his amorous experiences with the detached manner of a psychologist interested in the mental reactions of certain corporeal pleasures whose mechanism he has previously studied in his capacity of physiological observer. His attitude is the same as that of the writers of those comedies of manners which hold the stage in the theatres of the boulevards. It is dry, precise, matter-of-fact and almost scientific. The comedian of the boulevards does not concern himself with trying to find some sort of metaphysical justification for the raptures of physical passion, nor is he in any way a propagandist of sensuality. He is simply an analyst of facts, whose business it is to get all the wit that is possible out of an equivocal situation. Similarly, the author of these poems is

far too highly sophisticated to imagine
that

> every spirit as it is most pure,
> And hath in it the more of heavenly light,
> So it the fairer body doth procure
> To habit in, and it more fairly dight
> With cheerful grace and amiable sight.
> For of the soul the body form doth take ;
> For soul is form and doth the body make.

He does not try to make us believe that
physical pleasures have a divine justification. Neither has he any wish to " make
us grovel, hand and foot in Belial's gripe."
He is merely engaged in remembering
" des heures et des entretiens " which were
extremely pleasant—hours which strike
for every one, conversations and meetings
which are taking place in all parts of the
world and at every moment.

This attitude towards *volupté* is sufficiently old in France to have made
possible the evolution of a very precise
and definite vocabulary in which to describe its phenomena. This language is
as exact as the technical jargon of a trade,
and as elegant as the Latin of Petronius.
It is a language of which we have no
equivalent in our English literature. It
is impossible in English to describe *volupté*

elegantly; it is hardly possible to write of it without being gross. To begin with, we do not even possess a word equivalent to *volupté*. "Voluptuousness" is feeble and almost meaningless; "pleasure" is hopelessly inadequate. From the first the English writer is at a loss; he cannot even name precisely the thing he proposes to describe and analyse. But for the most part he has not much use for such a language. His approach to the subject is not dispassionate and scientific, and he has no need for technicalities. The English amorist is inclined to approach the subject rapturously, passionately, philosophically—almost in any way that is not the wittily matter-of-fact French way.

In our rich Australian *Songs of Love and Life* we see the rapturous-philosophic approach reduced to something that is very nearly the absurd. Overcome with the intensities of connubial bliss, the authoress feels it necessary to find a sort of justification for them by relating them in some way with the cosmos. God, we are told,

> looking through His hills on you and me,
> Feeds Heaven upon the flame of our desire.

NATIONALITY IN LOVE

Or again :

Our passions breathe their own wild harmony,
And pour out music at a clinging kiss.
Sing on, O Soul, our lyric of desire,
For God Himself is in the melody.

Meanwhile the author of *Les Baisers*,
always elegantly *terre-à-terre*, formulates
his more concrete desires in an Alexandrine
worthy of Racine :

Viens. Je veux dégrafer moi-même ton corsage.

The desire to involve the cosmos in
our emotions is by no means confined to
the poetess of *Songs of Love and Life*.
In certain cases we are all apt to invoke
the universe in an attempt to explain
and account for emotions whose intensity
seems almost inexplicable. This is particularly true of the emotions aroused in
us by the contemplation of beauty. Why
we should feel so strongly when confronted with certain forms and colours,
certain sounds, certain verbal suggestions
of form and harmony—why the thing
which we call beauty should move us at
all—goodness only knows. In order to
explain the phenomenon, poets have involved the universe in the matter, assert-

ing that they are moved by the contemplation of physical beauty because it is the symbol of the divine. The intensities of physical passion have presented the same problem. Ashamed of admitting that such feelings can have a purely sublunary cause, we affirm, like the Australian poetess, that " God Himself is in the melody." That, we argue, can be the only explanation for the violence of the emotion. This view of the matter is particularly common in a country with fundamental puritanic traditions like England, where the dry, matter-of-fact attitude of the French seems almost shocking. The puritan feels bound to justify the facts of beauty and *volupté*. They must be in some way made moral before he can accept them. The French un-puritanic mind accepts the facts as they are tendered to it by experience, at their face value.

HOW THE DAYS DRAW IN!

THE autumn equinox is close upon us with all its presages of mortality, a shortening day, a colder and longer night. How the days draw in ! Fear of ridicule hardly allows one to make the melancholy constatation. It is a conversational gambit that, like fool's mate, can only be used against the simplest and least experienced of players. And yet how much of the world's most moving poetry is nothing but a variation on the theme of this in-drawing day ! The certainty of death has inspired more poetry than the hope of immortality. The visible transience of frail and lovely matter has impressed itself more profoundly on the mind of man than the notion of spiritual permanence.

Et l'on verra bientôt surgir du sein de l'onde
La première clarté de mon dernier soleil.

That is an article of faith from which nobody can withhold assent.

Of late I have found myself almost incapable of enjoying any poetry whose inspiration is not despair or melancholy. Why, I hardly know. Perhaps it is due to the chronic horror of the political situation. For heaven knows, that is quite sufficient to account for a taste for melancholy verse. The subject of any European government to-day feels all the sensations of Gulliver in the paws of the Queen of Brobdingnag's monkey—the sensations of some small and helpless being at the mercy of something monstrous and irresponsible and idiotic. There sits the monkey " on the ridge of a building five hundred yards above the ground, holding us like a baby in one of his fore paws." Will he let go ? Will he squeeze us to death ? The best we can hope for is to be " let drop on a ridge tile," with only enough bruises to keep one in bed for a fortnight. But it seems very unlikely that some " honest lad will climb up and, putting us in his breeches pocket, bring us down safe." However, I divagate a little from my subject, which is the poetry of melancholy.

Some day I shall compile an Oxford Book of Depressing Verse, which shall contain nothing but the most magnificent expressions of melancholy and despair. All the obvious people will be in it and as many of the obscure apostles

of gloom as vague and miscellaneous
reading shall have made known to me.
A duly adequate amount of space, for
example, will be allotted to that all but
great poet, Fulke Greville, Lord Brooke.
For dark magnificence there are not
many things that can rival that summing
up against life and human destiny at the
end of his " Mustapha."

Oh wearisome condition of humanity,
Born under one law to another bound,
Vainly begot and yet forbidden vanity,
Created sick, commanded to be sound.
   What meaneth nature by these diverse
     laws,
   Passion and reason, self-division's cause ?

Is it the mark or majesty of power
To make offences that it may forgive ?
Nature herself doth her own self deflower
To hate those errors she herself doth give. . . .
   If nature did not take delight in blood,
   She would have made more easy ways to
    good.

Milton aimed at justifying the ways of
God to man ; Fulke Greville gloomily
denounces them.

Nor shall I omit from my anthology
the extraordinary description in the Pro-

logue to " Alaham " of the Hell of Hells
and of Privation, the peculiar torment of
the place :

Thou monster horrible, under whose ugly
    doom
Down in eternity's perpetual night
Man's temporal sins bear torments infinite,
For change of desolation must I come
To tempt the earth and to profane the light.
A place there is, upon no centre placed,
Deep under depths as far as is the sky
Above the earth, dark, infinitely spaced,
Pluto the king, the kingdom misery.
Privation would reign there, by God not made,
But creature of uncreated sin,
Whose being is all beings to invade,
To have no ending though it did begin ;
And so of past, things present and to come,
To give depriving, not tormenting doom.
But horror in the understanding mixed. . . .

Like most of his contemporaries in those
happy days before the notion of progress
had been invented, Lord Brooke was
what Peacock would have called a
" Pejorationist." His political views (and
they were also Sidney's) are reflected
in his *Life of Sir Philip Sidney*. The
best that a statesman can do, according
to these Elizabethan pessimists, is to
patch and prop the decaying fabric of

society in the hope of staving off for
a little longer the final inevitable crash.
It seems curious to us, who have learnt to
look at the Elizabethan age as the most
splendid in English history, that the
men who were the witnesses of these
splendours should have regarded their
time as an age of decadence.

The notion of the Fall was fruitful
in despairing poetry. One of the most
remarkable products of this doctrine is
a certain " Sonnet Chrétien " by the
seventeenth-century writer Jean Ogier
de Gombauld, surnamed " le Beau
Ténébreux."

Cette source de mort, cette homicide peste,
Ce péché dont l'enfer a le monde infecté,
M'a laissé pour tout être un bruit d'avoir été,
Et je suis de moi-même une image funeste.
L'Auteur de l'univers, le Monarque céleste
S'était rendu visible en ma seule beauté.
Ce vieux titre d'honneur qu'autrefois j'ai porté
Et que je porte encore, est tout ce qui me
    reste.

Mais c'est fait de ma gloire, et je ne suis plus
    rien
Qu'un fantôme qui court après l'ombre d'un
    bien,
Ou qu'un corps animé du seul ver qui le ronge.

Non, je ne suis plus rien quand je veux
 m'éprouver,
Qu'un esprit ténébreux qui voit tout comme
 en songe
Et cherche incessament ce qu'il ne peut trouver.

There are astonishing lines in this, lines that might have been written by a Baudelaire, if he had been born a Huguenot and two hundred years before his time. That "carcase animated by the sole gnawing worm" is something that one would expect to find rotting away among the sombre and beautiful Flowers of Evil.

An amusing speculation. If Steinach's rejuvenating operations on the old become the normal and accepted thing, what will be the effect on poetry of this abolition of the depressing process of decay? It may be that the poetry of melancholy and despair is destined to lose its place in literature, and that a spirit of what William James called "healthy-mindedness" will inherit its kingdom. Many "eternal truths" have already found their way on to the dust-heap of antiquated ideas. It may be that this last and seemingly most inexorable of them—that life is short and subject to a dreadful

decay—will join the other great common-
places which have already perished out of
literature.

> The flesh is bruckle, the fiend is slee :
> Timor mortis conturbat me :—

Some day, it may be, these sentiments
will seem as hopelessly superannuated as
Milton's cosmology.

TIBET

IN moments of complete despair, when it seems that all is for the worst in the worst of all possible worlds, it is cheering to discover that there are places where stupidity reigns even more despotically than in Western Europe, where civilization is based on principles even more fantastically unreasonable. Recent experience has shown me that the depression into which the Peace, Mr. Churchill, the state of contemporary literature, have conspired to plunge the mind, can be sensibly relieved by a study, even superficial, of the manners and customs of Tibet. The spectacle of an ancient and elaborate civilization of which almost no detail is not entirely idiotic is in the highest degree comforting and refreshing. It fills us with hopes of the ultimate success of our own civilization ; it restores our wavering self-satisfaction in being citizens of industrialized Europe. Compared with Tibet, we are prodigious. Let us cherish the comparison.

My informant about Tibetan civilization is a certain Japanese monk of the name of Kawaguchi, who spent three years in Tibet at the beginning of the present century. His account of the experience has been translated into English, and published, with the title *Three Years in Tibet*, by the Theosophical Society. It is one of the great travel books of the world, and, so far as I am aware, the most interesting book on Tibet that exists. Kawaguchi enjoyed opportunities in Tibet which no European traveller could possibly have had. He attended the University of Lhasa, he enjoyed the acquaintance of the Dalai Lama himself, he was intimate with one of the four Ministers of Finance, he was the friend of lama and layman, of all sorts and conditions of Tibetans, from the highest class to the lowest—the despicable caste of smiths and butchers. He knew his Tibet intimately; for those three years, indeed, he was for all practical purposes a Tibetan. This is something which no European explorer can claim, and it is this which gives Kawaguchi's book its unique interest.

The Japanese, like people of every other nationality except the Chinese, are not permitted to enter Tibet. Mr. Kawaguchi did not allow this to stand in the way of his pious mission—for his purpose

in visiting Tibet was to investigate the
Buddhist writings and traditions of the
place. He made his way to India, and
in a long stay at Darjeeling familiarized
himself with the Tibetan language. He
then set out to walk across the Himalayas.
Not daring to affront the strictly guarded
gates which bar the direct route to
Lhasa, he penetrated Tibet at its south-
western corner, underwent prodigious
hardships in an uninhabited desert
eighteen thousand feet above sea-level,
visited the holy lake of Manosarovara,
and finally, after astonishing adventures,
arrived in Lhasa. Here he lived for
nearly three years, passing himself off
as a Chinaman. At the end of that time
his secret leaked out, and he was obliged
to accelerate his departure for India.
So much for Kawaguchi himself, though
I should have liked to say more of him ;
for a more charming and sympathetic
character never revealed himself in a
book.

Tibet is so full of fantastic low comedy
that one hardly knows where to begin a
catalogue of its absurdities. Shall we
start with the Tibetans' highly organized
service of trained nurses, whose sole

duty it is to prevent their patients from going to sleep ? or with the Dalai Lama's chief source of income—the sale of pills made of dung, at, literally, a guinea a box ? or with the Tibetan custom of never washing from the moment of birth, when, however, they are plentifully anointed with melted butter, to the moment of death ? And then there is the University of Lhasa, which an eminent Cambridge philosopher has compared with the University of Oxford—somewhat unjustly, perhaps ; but let that pass. At the University of Lhasa the student is instructed in logic and philosophy ; every year of his stay he has to learn by heart from one to five or six hundred pages of holy texts. He is also taught mathematics, but in Tibet this art is not carried farther than subtraction. It takes twenty years to get a degree at the University of Lhasa—twenty years, and then most of the candidates are ploughed. To obtain a superior Ph.D. degree, entitling one to become a really holy and eminent lama, forty years of application to study and to virtue are required. But it is useless to try to make a catalogue of the delights of Tibet.

There are too many of them for mention in this small space. One can do no more than glance at a few of the brighter spots in the system.

There is much to be said for the Tibetan system of taxation. The Government requires a considerable revenue ; for enormous sums have to be spent in keeping perpetually burning in the principal Buddhist cathedral of Lhasa an innumerable army of lamps, which may not be fed with anything cheaper than clarified yak butter. This is the heaviest item of expenditure. But a great deal of money also goes to supporting the Tibetan clergy, who must number at least a sixth of the total population. The money is raised by a poll tax, paid in kind, the amount of which, fixed by ancient tradition, may, theoretically, never be altered. Theoretically only ; for the Tibetan Government employs in the collection of taxes no fewer than twenty different standards of weight and thirty-six different standards of measure. The pound may weigh anything from half to a pound and a half ; and the same with the units of measure. It is thus possible to calculate with extraordinary nicety, according to the standard of weight and measure in which your tax is assessed, where precisely you stand in the Government's favour. If you are a notoriously bad character, or even if you are innocent, but live in a bad district, your tax will have to be paid in measures of the largest size. If you are virtuous, or, better, if you are rich, of good family and *bien pensant*, then you will pay by weights which are only half the nominal weight. For those whom the Government neither hates nor loves, but regards with more or less contempt or tolerance, there are the thirty-four intervening degrees.

Kawaguchi's final judgment of the Tibetans, after three years' intimate acquaintance with them, is not a flattering one :

The Tibetans are characterized by four serious defects, these being : filthiness, superstition, unnatural customs (such as polyandry), and unnatural art. I should be sorely perplexed if I were asked to name their redeeming points ; but if I had to do so, I should mention first of all the fine climate in the vicinity of Lhasa and Shigatze, their sonorous and refreshing voices in reading the Text, the animated style of their catechisms, and their ancient art.

Certainly a bad lot of vices ; but then the Tibetan virtues are not lightly to be set aside. We English possess none of them : our climate is abominable, our method of reading the holy texts is painful in the extreme, our catechisms, at least in my young days, were far from animated, and our ancient art is very indifferent stuff. But still, in spite of these defects, in spite of Mr. Churchill and the state of contemporary literature, we can still look at the Tibetans and feel reassured.

BEAUTY IN 1920

TO those who know how to read the signs of the times it will have become apparent, in the course of these last days and weeks, that the Silly Season is close upon us. Already—and this in July with the menace of three or four new wars grumbling on the thunderous horizon—already a monster of the deep has appeared at a popular seaside resort. Already Mr. Louis McQuilland has launched in the *Daily Express* a fierce onslaught on the younger poets of the Asylum. Already the picture-papers are more than half filled with photographs of bathing nymphs—photographs that make one understand the ease with which St. Anthony rebuffed his temptations. The newspaper-men, ramping up and down like wolves, seek their prey wherever they may find it ; and it was with a unanimous howl of delight that the whole Press went pelting after the hare started by Mrs. Asquith in a recent instalment of her autobiography. Feebly and belatedly, let me follow the pack.

Mrs. Asquith's denial of beauty to the daughters of the twentieth century has proved a god-sent giant gooseberry. It has necessitated the calling in of a whole host of skin-food specialists, portrait-painters and photographers to deny this far from soft impeachment. A great deal of space has been agreeably and inexpensively filled. Every one is satisfied—public, editors, skin-food specialists and all. But by far the most interesting contribution to the debate was a pictorial one, which appeared, if I remember rightly, in the *Daily News*. Side by side, on the same page, we were shown the photographs of three beauties of the eighteen-eighties and three of the nineteen-twenties. The comparison was most instructive. For a great gulf separates the two types of beauty represented by these two sets of photographs.

I remember in *If*, one of those charming conspiracies of E. V. Lucas and George Morrow, a series of parodied fashion-plates entitled " If Faces get any Flatter. Last year's standard, this year's Evening Standard." The faces of our living specimens of beauty have grown flatter with those of their fashion-plate sisters. Compare the types of 1880 and 1920. The first is steep-faced, almost Roman in profile ; in the contemporary

116

beauties the face has broadened and
shortened, the profile is less noble, less
imposing, more appealingly, more allur-
ingly pretty. Forty years ago it was the
aristocratic type that was appreciated;
to-day the popular taste has shifted from
the countess to the soubrette. Photog-
raphy confirms the fact that the ladies
of the 'eighties looked like Du Maurier
drawings. But among the present young
generation one looks in vain for the type;
the Du Maurier damsel is as extinct as
the mesozoic reptile; the Fish girl and
other kindred flat-faced species have taken
her place.

Between the 'thirties and 'fifties another type, the egg-faced girl, reigned
supreme in the affections of the world.
From the early portraits of Queen Victoria
to the fashion-plates in the *Ladies' Keep-
sake* this invariable type prevails—the
egg-shaped face, the sleek hair, the swan-
like neck, the round, champagne-bottle
shoulders. Compared with the decorous
impassivity of the oviform girl our flat-
faced fashion-plates are terribly abandoned
and provocative. And because one ex-
pects so much in the way of respectability
from these egg-faces of an earlier age,

one is apt to be shocked when one sees them conducting themselves in ways that seem unbefitting. One thinks of that enchanting picture of Etty's, " Youth on the Prow and Pleasure at the Helm." The naiads are of the purest egg-faced type. Their hair is sleek, their shoulders slope and their faces are as impassive as blanks. And yet they have no clothes on. It is almost indecent ; one imagined that the egg-faced type came into the world complete with flowing draperies.

It is not only the face of beauty that alters with the changes of popular taste. The champagne-bottle shoulders of the oviform girl have vanished from the modern fashion-plate and from modern life. The contemporary hand, with its two middle fingers held together and the forefinger and little finger splayed apart, is another recent product. Above all, the feet have changed. In the days of the egg-faces no fashion-plate had more than one foot. This rule will, I think, be found invariable. That solitary foot projects, generally in a strangely haphazard way as though it had nothing to do with a leg, from under the edge of the skirt. And what a foot ! It has no relation to those provocative feet in Suckling's ballad :

> Her feet beneath her petticoat
> Like little mice stole in and out.

It is an austere foot. It is a small, black, oblong object like a tea-leaf. No living human being has ever seen a foot like it, for it is utterly unlike the feet of nineteen-twenty. To-day the fashion-plate is always a biped. The tea-leaf has been replaced by two feet of rich baroque design, curved and florid, with insteps like the necks of Arab horses. Faces may have changed shape, but feet have altered far more radically. On the text, " the feet of the young women," it would be possible to write a profound philo-sophical sermon.

And while I am on the subject of feet I would like to mention another curious phenomenon of the same kind, but affect-ing, this time, the standards of male beauty. Examine the pictorial art of the eighteenth century, and you will find that the shape of the male leg is not what it was. In those days the calf of the leg was not a muscle that bulged to its greatest dimensions a little below the back of the knee, to subside, *decrescendo*, towards the ankle. No, in the eighteenth century the calf was an even crescent, with its greatest projection opposite the middle of the shin; the ankle, as we know it, hardly existed. This curious calf is forced upon one's attention by almost every minor picture-maker of the eighteenth century, and even by some of the great masters, as, for instance, Blake. How it came into existence I do not know. Presumably the crescent calf was considered, in the art schools, to approach more nearly to the Platonic Idea of the human leg than did the poor distorted Appearance of real life. Personally, I prefer my calves with the bulge at the top and a proper ankle at the bottom. But then I don't hold much with the *beau idéal*.

The process by which one type of beauty becomes popular, imposes its tyranny for a period and then is displaced by a dissimilar type is a mysterious one. It may be that patient historical scholars will end by discovering some law to explain the transformation of the Du Maurier type into the flat-face type, the tea-leaf foot into the baroque foot, the crescent calf into the normal calf. As far as one can see at present, these changes seem to be the result of mere hazard and arbitrary choice. But a time will doubtless come when it will be found that these changes of taste are as ineluctably predetermined as any chemical change. Given the South African War, the accession of Edward VII. and the Liberal triumph of 1906, it was, no doubt, as inevitable that Du Maurier should have given place to Fish as that zinc subjected to sulphuric acid should break up into $ZnSO_4 + H_2$. But we leave it to others to formulate the precise workings of the law.

GREAT THOUGHTS

TO all lovers of unfamiliar quotations, aphorisms, great thoughts and intellectual gems, I would heartily recommend a heavy volume recently published in Brussels and entitled *Pensées sur la Science, la Guerre et sur des sujets très variés.* The book contains some twelve or thirteen thousand quotations, selected from a treasure of one hundred and twenty-three thousand great thoughts gleaned and garnered by the industry of Dr. Maurice Legat—an industry which will be appreciated at its value by any one who has ever made an attempt to compile a commonplace book or private anthology of his own. The almost intolerable labour of copying out extracts can only be avoided by the drastic use of the scissors ; and there are few who can afford the luxury of mutilating their copies of the best authors.

For some days I made Dr. Legat's book my *livre de chevet.* But I had very soon to give up reading it at night, for I found that the Great often said things so peculiar that I was kept awake in the effort to discover their meaning. Why, for example, should it be categorically stated by Lamennais that " si les animaux connaissaient Dieu, ils parleraient " ? What could Cardinal Maury have meant when he said, " L'éloquence, compagne ordinaire de la liberté [astonishing generalization !], est inconnue en Angleterre " ? These were mysteries insoluble enough to counteract the soporific effects of such profound truths as this, discovered, apparently, in 1846 by Monsieur C. H. D. Duponchel, " Le plus sage mortel est sujet à l'erreur."

Dr. Legat has found some pleasing quotations on the subject of England and the English. His selection proves with what fatal ease even the most intelligent minds are lured into making generalizations about national character, and how grotesque those generalizations always are. Montesquieu informs us that " dès que sa fortune se délabre, un anglais tue ou se fait voleur." Of the better half of this potential murderer and robber Balzac says, " La femme anglaise est une pauvre créature verteuse par force, prête à se dépraver." " La vanité est l'âme de toute société anglaise," says Lamartine. Ledru - Rollin is of opinion that all the riches of England are " des dépouilles volées aux tombeaux."

The Goncourts risk a characteristically dashing generalization on the national characters of England and France : " L'Anglais, filou comme peuple, est honnête comme individu. Il est le contraire du Français, honnête comme peuple, et filou comme individu." If one is going to make a comparison Voltaire's is more satisfactory because less pretentious. Strange are the ways of you Englishmen,

> qui, des mêmes couteaux,
> Coupez la tête au roi et la queue aux chevaux.
> Nous Français, plus humains, laissons aux rois
> leurs têtes,
> Et la queue à nos bêtes.

It is unfortunate that history should have vitiated the truth of this pithy and pregnant statement.

But the bright spots in this enormous tome are rare. After turning over a few hundred pages one is compelled, albeit reluctantly, to admit that the Great Thought or Maxim is nearly the most boring form of literature that exists. Others, it seems, have anticipated me in this grand discovery. " Las de m'ennuyer des pensées des autres," says d'Alembert, "j'ai voulu leur donner les miennes ; mais je puis me flatter de leur avoir rendu tout l'ennui que j'avais reçu d'eux." Almost next to d'Alembert's statement I find this confession from the pen of J. Roux (1834–1906) : " Emettre des pensées, voilà ma consolation, mon délice, ma vie ! " Happy Monsieur Roux !

Turning dissatisfied from Dr. Legat's anthology of thought, I happened upon the second number of *Proverbe*, a monthly review, four pages in length, directed by M. Paul Eluard and counting among its contributors Tristan Tzara of *Dada* fame, Messrs. Soupault, Breton and Aragon, the directors of *Littérature*, M. Picabia, M. Ribemont-Dessaignes and others of the same kidney. Here, on the front page of the March number of *Proverbe*, I found the very comment on Great Thoughts for which I had, in my dissatisfaction, been looking. The following six maxims are printed one below the other : the first of them is a quotation from the *Intransigeant* ; the other five appear to be the work of M. Tzara, who appends a footnote to this effect : " Je m'appelle dorénavant exclusivement

Monsieur Paul Bourget." Here they
are :

Il faut violer les règles, oui, mais pour les
violer il faut les connaître.

Il faut régler la connaissance, oui, mais pour
la régler il faut la violer.

Il faut connaître les viols, oui, mais pour les
connaître il faut les régler.

Il faut connaître les règles, oui, mais pour les
connaître il faut les violer.

Il faut régler les viols, oui, mais pour les
régler il faut les connaître.

Il faut violer la connaissance, oui, mais pour
la violer il faut la régler.

It is to be hoped that Dr. Legat will
find room for at least a selection of these
profound thoughts in the next edition
of his book. " LE passé et LA pensée
n'existent pas," affirms M. Raymond
Duncan on another page of *Proverbe*.
It is precisely after taking too large a
dose of " Pensées sur la Science, la Guerre
et sur des sujets très variés " that one
half wishes the statement were in fact
true.

ADVERTISEMENT

I HAVE always been interested in the subtleties of literary form. This preoccupation with the outward husk, with the letter of literature, is, I dare say, the sign of a fundamental spiritual impotence. Gigadibs, the literary man, can understand the tricks of the trade ; but when it is a question, not of conjuring, but of miracles, he is no more effective than Mr. Sludge. Still, conjuring is amusing to watch and to practise ; an interest in the machinery of the art requires no further justification. I have dallied with many literary forms, taking pleasure in their different intricacies, studying the means by which great authors of the past have resolved the technical problems presented by each. Sometimes I have even tried my hand at solving the problems myself—delightful and salubrious exercise for the mind. And now I have discovered the most exciting, the most arduous literary form of all, the most difficult to master, the most pregnant in curious possibilities. I mean the advertisement.

Nobody who has not tried to write an advertisement has any idea of the delights and difficulties presented by this form of literature—or shall I say of " applied literature," for the sake of those who still believe in the romantic superiority of the pure, the disinterested, over the immediately useful ? The problem that confronts the writer of advertisements is an immensely complicated one, and by reason of its very arduousness immensely interesting. It is far easier to write ten passably effective Sonnets, good enough to take in the not too inquiring critic, than one effective advertisement that will take in a few thousand of the uncritical buying public. The problem presented by the Sonnet is child's play compared with the problem of the advertisement. In writing a Sonnet one need think only of oneself. If one's readers find one boring or obscure, so much the worse for them. But in writing an advertisement one must think of other people. Advertisement writers may not be lyrical, or obscure, or in any way esoteric. They must be universally intelligible. A good advertisement has this in common with drama and oratory, that it must be immediately comprehensible and directly moving. But at the same time it must possess all the succinctness of epigram.

The orator and the dramatist have "world enough and time" to produce their effects by cumulative appeals; they can turn all round their subject, they can repeat; between the heights of their eloquence they can gracefully practise the art of sinking, knowing that a period of flatness will only set off the splendour of their impassioned moments. But the advertiser has no space to spare; he pays too dearly for every inch. He must play upon the minds of his audience with a small and limited instrument. He must persuade them to part with their money in a speech that is no longer than many a lyric by Herrick. Could any problem be more fascinatingly difficult? No one should be allowed to talk about the *mot juste* or the polishing of style who has not tried his hand at writing an advertisement of something which the public does not want, but which it must be persuaded into buying. Your *boniment* must not exceed a poor hundred and fifty or two hundred words. With what care you must weigh every syllable! What infinite pains must be taken to fashion every phrase into a barbed hook that shall stick in the reader's mind and draw from its hiding-place within his pocket the reluctant coin! One's style and ideas must be lucid and simple enough to be understood by all; but, at the same time, they must not be vulgar. Elegance and an economical distinction are required; but any trace of literariness in an advertisement is fatal to its success.

I do not know whether any one has yet written a history of advertising. If the book does not already exist it will certainly have to be written. The story of the development of advertising from its infancy in the early nineteenth century to its luxuriant maturity in the twentieth is an essential chapter in the history of democracy. Advertisement begins abjectly, crawling on its belly like the serpent after the primal curse. Its abjection is the oily humbleness of the shopkeeper in an oligarchical society. Those nauseating references to the nobility and clergy, which are the very staple of early advertisements, are only possible in an age when the aristocracy and its established Church effectively ruled the land. The custom of invoking these powers lingered on long after they had ceased to hold sway. It is now, I fancy, almost wholly extinct. It may be that certain old-fashioned girls' schools still provide education for the daughters of the nobility and clergy; but I am inclined to doubt it. Advertisers still find it worth while to parade the names and escutcheons of kings. But anything less than royalty is, frankly, a " wash-out."

The crawling style of advertisement with its mixture of humble appeals to patrons and its hyperbolical laudation of the goods advertised, was early varied by the pseudo-scientific style, a simple development of the quack's patter at the fair. Balzacians will remember the advertisement composed by Finot and the Illustrious Gaudissard for César Birotteau's " Huile Céphalique." The type is not yet dead; we still see advertisements of substances " based on the principles established by the Academy of Sciences," substances known " to the ancients, the Romans, the Greeks and the nations of the North," but lost and only rediscovered by the advertiser. The style and manner of these advertisements belonging to the early and middle periods of the Age of Advertisement continue to bear the imprint of the once despicable position of commerce. They are written with the impossible and insincere unctuousness of tradesmen's letters. They are horribly uncultured; and when their writers aspire to something more ambitious than the counting-house style, they fall at once into the stilted verbiage of self-taught learning. Some of the earlier efforts to raise the tone of advertisements are very curious. One remembers those remarkable full-page advertisements of Eno's Fruit Salt, loaded with weighty apophthegms from Emerson, Epictetus, Zeno the Eleatic, Pomponazzi, Slawkenbergius and other founts of human wisdom. There was noble reading on these strange pages. But they shared with sermons the defect of being a little dull.

The art of advertisement writing has flowered with democracy. The lords of industry and commerce came gradually to understand that the right way to appeal to the Free Peoples of the World was familiarly, in an honest man-to-man style. They perceived that exaggeration and hyperbole do not really pay, that charlatanry must at least have an air of sincerity. They confided in the public, they appealed to its intelligence in every kind of flattering way. The technique of the art became at once immensely more difficult than it had ever been before, until now the advertisement is, as I have already hinted, one of the most interesting and difficult of modern literary forms. Its potentialities are not yet half explored. Already the most interesting and, in some cases, the only readable part of most American periodicals is the advertisement section. What does the future hold in store ?

EUPHUES REDIVIVUS

I HAVE recently been fortunate in securing a copy of that very rare and precious novel *Delina Delaney*, by Amanda M. Ros, authoress of *Irene Iddesleigh* and *Poems of Puncture*. Mrs. Ros's name is only known to a small and select band of readers. But by these few she is highly prized ; one of her readers, it is said, actually was at the pains to make a complete manuscript copy of *Delina Delaney*, so great was his admiration and so hopelessly out of print the book. Let me recommend the volume, Mrs. Ros's masterpiece, to the attention of enterprising publishers.

Delina Delaney opens with a tremendous, an almost, in its richness of vituperative eloquence, Rabelaisian denunciation of Mr. Barry Pain, who had, it seems, treated *Irene Iddesleigh* with scant respect in his review of the novel in *Black and White*. " This so-called Barry Pain, by name, has taken upon himself to criticize a work, the depth of which fails to reach the solving power of his borrowed, and, he'd have you believe, varied talent." But " I care not for the opinion of half-starved upstarts, who don the garb of a shabby-genteel, and fain would feed the mind of the people with the worthless scraps of stolen fancies." So perish all reviewers! And now for Delina herself.

The story is a simple one. Delina Delaney, daughter of a fisherman, loves and is loved by Lord Gifford. The baleful influence of a dark-haired French-woman, Madame de Maine, daughter of the Count-av-Nevo, comes between the lovers and their happiness, and Delina undergoes fearful torments, including three years' penal servitude, before their union can take place. It is the manner, rather than the matter, of the book which is remarkable. Here, for instance, is a fine conversation between Lord Gifford and his mother, an aristocratic dame who strenuously objects to his connection with Delina. Returning one day to Columba Castle she hears an unpleasant piece of news : her son has been seen kissing Delina in the conservatory.

" Home again, mother ? " he boldly uttered, as he gazed reverently in her face.

" Home to Hades ! " returned the raging high-bred daughter of distinguished effeminacy.

"Ah me! what is the matter?" meekly inquired his lordship.

"Everything is the matter with a broken-hearted mother of low-minded offspring," she answered hotly. . . . "Henry Edward Ludlow Gifford, son of my strength, idolized remnant of my inert husband, who at this moment invisibly offers the scourging whip of fatherly authority to your backbone of resentment (though for years you think him dead to your movements) and pillar of maternal trust."

Poor Lady Gifford! her son's behaviour was her undoing. The shock caused her to lose first her reason and then her life. Her son was heart-broken at the thought that he was responsible for her downfall:

"Is it true, O Death," I cried in my agony, "that you have wrested from me my mother, Lady Gifford of Columba Castle, and left me here, a unit figuring on the great blackboard of the past, the shaky surface of the present and fickle field of the future to track my life-steps, with gross indifference to her wished-for wish?" . . . Blind she lay to the presence of her son, who charged her death-gun with the powder of accelerated wrath.

It is impossible to suppose that Mrs. Ros can ever have read *Euphues* or the earlier romances of Robert Greene. How then shall we account for the extra-ordinary resemblance to Euphuism of her style? how explain those rich alliterations, those elaborate " kennings " and circumlocutions of which the fabric of her book is woven? Take away from Lyly his erudition and his passion for antithesis, and you have Mrs. Ros. Delina is own sister to Euphues and Pandosto. The fact is that Mrs. Ros happens, though separated from Euphuism by three hundred years and more, to have arrived independently at precisely the same stage of development as Lyly and his disciples. It is possible to see in a growing child a picture in miniature of all the phases through which humanity has passed in its development. And, in the same way, the mind of an individual (especially when that individual has been isolated from the main current of contemporary thought) may climb, alone, to a point at which, in the past, a whole generation has rested. In Mrs. Ros we see, as we see in the Elizabethan novelists, the result of the discovery of art by an unsophisticated mind and of its first conscious attempt to produce the artistic. It is remarkable how late in the history

of every literature simplicity is invented.
The first attempts of any people to be
consciously literary are always productive of the most elaborate artificiality.
Poetry is always written before prose
and always in a language as remote as
possible from the language of ordinary
life. The language and versification of
" Beowulf " are far more artificial and
remote from life than those of, say, *The
Rape of the Lock*. The Euphuists were
not barbarians making their first discovery
of literature ; they were, on the contrary,
highly educated. But in one thing they
were unsophisticated : they were discovering prose. They were realizing that
prose could be written with art, and they
wrote it as artificially as they possibly
could, just as their Saxon ancestors wrote
poetry. They became intoxicated with
their discovery of artifice. It was some
time before the intoxication wore off and
men saw that art was possible without
artifice. Mrs. Ros, an Elizabethan
born out of her time, is still under
the spell of that magical and delicious
intoxication.

Mrs. Ros's artifices are often more remarkable and elaborate even than Lyly's.

EUPHUES REDIVIVUS

This is how she tells us that Delina earned money by doing needlework :

She tried hard to keep herself a stranger to her poor old father's slight income by the use of the finest production of steel, whose blunt edge eyed the reely covering with marked greed, and offered its sharp dart to faultless fabrics of flaxen fineness.

And Lord Gifford parts from Delina in these words :

I am just in time to hear the toll of a parting bell strike its heavy weight of appalling softness against the weakest fibres of a heart of love, arousing and tickling its dormant action, thrusting the dart of evident separation deeper into its tubes of tenderness, and fanning the flame, already unextinguishable, into volumes of burning blaze.

But more often Mrs. Ros does not exceed the bounds which Lyly set for himself. Here, for instance, is a sentence that might have come direct out of *Euphues* :

Two days after, she quit Columba Castle and resolved to enter the holy cloisters of a convent, where, she believed she'd be dead to the built hopes of wealthy worth, the crooked steps to worldly distinction, and the designing creaks [*sic*] in the muddy stream of love.

Or again, this description of the artful charmers who flaunt along the streets of London is written in the very spirit and language of *Euphues* :

Their hair was a light-golden colour, thickly fringed in front, hiding in many cases the furrows of a life of vice ; behind, reared coils, some of which differed in hue, exhibiting the fact that they were on patrol for the price of another supply of dye. . . . The elegance of their attire had the glow of robbery—the rustle of many a lady's silent curse. These tools of brazen effrontery were strangers to the blush of innocence that tinged many a cheek, as they would gather round some of God's ordained, praying in flowery words of decoying Cockney, that they should break their holy vows by accompanying them to the halls of adultery. Nothing daunted at the staunch refusal of different divines, whose modest walk was interrupted by their bold assertion of loathsome rights, they moved on, while laughs of hidden rage and defeat flitted across their doll-decked faces, to die as they next accosted some rustic-looking critics, who, tempted with their polished twang, their earnest advances, their pitiful entreaties, yielded, in their ignorance of the ways of a large city, to their glossy offers, and accompanied, with slight hesitation, these artificial shells of immorality to their homes of ruin, degradation and shame.

THE AUTHOR OF "EMINENT VICTORIANS"

A SUPERLATIVELY civilized Red Indian living apart from the vulgar world in an elegant and park-like reservation, Mr. Strachey rarely looks over his walls at the surrounding country. It seethes, he knows, with crowds of horribly colonial persons. Like the hosts of Midian, the innumerable " poor whites " prowl and prowl around, but the noble savage pays no attention to them.

In his spiritual home—a neat and commodious Georgian mansion in the style of Leoni or Ware—he sits and reads, he turns over portfolios of queer old prints, he savours meditatively the literary vintages of centuries. And occasionally, once in two or three years, he tosses over his park palings a record of these leisured degustations, a judgment passed upon his library, a ripe rare book. One time it is Eminent Victorians ; the next it is Queen Victoria herself. To-day he has given us a miscellaneous collection of *Books and Characters*.

If Voltaire had lived to the age of two hundred and thirty instead of shuffling off at a paltry eighty-four, he would have written about the Victorian epoch, about life and letters at large, very much as Mr. Strachey has written. That lucid common sense, that sharp illuminating wit which delight us in the writings of the middle eighteenth century—these are Mr. Strachey's characteristics. We know exactly what he would have been if he had come into the world at the beginning of the seventeen hundreds ; if he is different from the men of that date it is because he happens to have been born towards the end of the eighteens.

The sum of knowledge at the disposal of the old Encyclopædists was singularly small, compared, that is to say, with the knowledge which we of the twentieth century have inherited. They made mistakes, and in their ignorance they passed what we can see to have been hasty and very imperfect judgments on men and things. Mr. Strachey is the eighteenth-century grown-up ; he is Voltaire at two hundred and thirty.

Voltaire at sixty would have treated the Victorian era, if it could have appeared in a prophetical vision before his eyes, in terms of " La Pucelle "—with ribaldry. He would have had to be much older in knowledge and inherited experience before he could have approached it in that spirit of sympathetic irony and ironical sympathy which Mr. Strachey brings to bear upon it. Mr. Strachey makes us like the old Queen, while we smile at her; he makes us admire the Prince Consort in spite of the portentous priggishness—duly insisted on in the biography—which accompanied his intelligence. With all the untutored barbarity of their notions, Gordon and Florence Nightingale are presented to us as sympathetic figures. Their peculiar brand of religion and ethics might be absurd, but their characters are shown to be interesting and fine.

It is only in the case of Dr. Arnold that Mr. Strachey permits himself to be unrestrainedly Voltairean; he becomes a hundred and seventy years younger as he describes the founder of the modern Public School system. The irony of that description is tempered by no sympathy. To make the man appear even more ridiculous, Mr. Strachey adds a stroke or two to the portrait of his own contriving —little inventions which deepen the absurdity of the caricature. Thus we

read that Arnold's " outward appearance
was the index of his inward character.
The legs, perhaps, were shorter than they
should have been ; but the sturdy athletic
frame, especially when it was swathed
(as it usually was) in the flowing robes
of a Doctor of Divinity, was full of an
imposing vigour." How exquisitely right
those short legs are ! how artistically
inevitable ! Our admiration for Mr.
Strachey's art is only increased when we
discover that in attributing to the Doctor
this brevity of shank he is justified by no
contemporary document. The short legs
are his own contribution.

Voltaire, then, at two hundred and
thirty has learned sympathy. He has
learned that there are other ways of
envisaging life than the common-sense,
reasonable way and that people with a
crack-brained view of the universe have
a right to be judged as human beings
and must not be condemned out of hand
as lunatics or obscurantists. Blake and
St. Francis have as much right to their
place in the sun as Gibbon and Hume.
But still, in spite of this lesson, learned
and inherited from the nineteenth century,
our Voltaire of eleven score years and

ten still shows a marked preference for the Gibbons and the Humes ; he still understands their attitude towards life a great deal better than he understands the other fellow's attitude.

In his new volume of *Books and Characters* Mr. Strachey prints an essay on Blake (written, it may be added parenthetically, some sixteen years ago), in which he sets out very conscientiously to give that disquieting poet his due. The essay is interesting, not because it contains anything particularly novel in the way of criticism, but because it reveals, in spite of all Mr. Strachey's efforts to overcome it, in spite of his admiration for the great artist in Blake, his profound antagonism towards Blake's view of life.

He cannot swallow mysticism ; he finds it clearly very difficult to understand what all this fuss about the soul really signifies. The man who believes in the absoluteness of good and evil, who sees the universe as a spiritual entity concerned, in some transcendental fashion, with morality, the man who regards the human spirit as possessing a somehow cosmic importance and significance—ah no, decidedly no, even at two hundred and thirty Voltaire cannot whole-heartedly sympathize with such a man.

And that, no doubt, is the reason why Mr. Strachey has generally shrunk from dealing, in his biographies and his criticisms, with any of these strange incomprehensible characters. Blake is the only one he has tried his hand on, and the result is not entirely satisfactory. He is more at home with the Gibbons and Humes of this world, and when he is not discussing the reasonable beings he likes to amuse himself with the eccentrics, like Mr. Creevey or Lady Hester Stanhope. The portentous, formidable mystics he leaves severely alone.

One cannot imagine Mr. Strachey coping with Dostoevsky or with any of the other great explorers of the soul. One cannot imagine him writing a life of Beethoven. These huge beings are disquieting for a Voltaire who has learned enough sympathy to be able to recognize their greatness, but whose temperament still remains unalterably alien. Mr. Strachey is wise to have nothing to do with them.

The second-rate mystics (I use the term in its widest and vaguest sense), the men who believe in the spirituality of the universe and in the queerer dogmas which have become tangled in that belief, without possessing the genius which alone can justify such notions in the eyes of the Voltaireans—these are the objects on which Mr. Strachey likes to turn his calm and penetrating gaze. Gordon and Florence Nightingale, the Prince Consort, Clough—they and their beliefs are made to look rather absurd by the time he has done with them. He reduces their spiritual struggles to a series of the most comically futile series of gymnastics in the void. The men of genius who have gone through the same spiritual struggles, who have believed the same sort of creeds, have had the unanswerable justification of their genius. These poor absurd creatures have not. Voltaire in his third century gives them a certain amount of his newly learned sympathy ; but he also gives them a pretty strong dose of his old irony.

EDWARD THOMAS[1]

THE poetry of Edward Thomas affects one morally as well as æsthetically and intellectually. We have grown rather shy, in these days of pure æstheticism, of speaking of those consoling or strengthening qualities of poetry on which critics of another generation took pleasure in dwelling. Thomas's poetry is strengthening and consoling, not because it justifies God's ways to man or whispers of reunions beyond the grave, not because it presents great moral truths in memorable numbers, but in a more subtle and very much more effective way. Walking through the streets on these September nights, one notices, wherever there are trees along the street and lamps close beside the trees, a curious and beautiful phenomenon. The light of the street lamps striking up into the trees has power to make the grimed, shabby, and tattered foliage of the all-but autumn seem brilliantly and transparently green. Within the magic circle of the light the tree seems to be at that crowning moment of the spring when the leaves are fully

[1] *Collected Poems*, by Edward Thomas: with a Foreword by W. de la Mare. Selwyn & Blount.

grown, but still luminous with youth and seemingly almost immaterial in their lightness. Thomas's poetry is to the mind what that transfiguring lamplight is to the tired trees. On minds grown weary in the midst of the intolerable turmoil and aridity of daily wage-earning existence, it falls with a touch of momentary rejuvenation.

The secret of Thomas's influence lies in the fact that he is genuinely what so many others of our time quite unjustifiably claim to be, a nature poet. To be a nature poet it is not enough to affirm vaguely that God made the country and man made the town, it is not enough to talk sympathetically about familiar rural objects, it is not enough to be sonorously poetical about mountains and trees ; it is not even enough to speak of these things with the precision of real knowledge and love. To be a nature poet a man must have felt profoundly and intimately those peculiar emotions which nature can inspire, and must be able to express them in such a way that his reader feels them. The real difficulty that confronts the would-be poet of nature is that these emotions are of all emotions the most difficult to pin down and analyse, and the hardest of all to convey. In " October" Thomas describes what is surely the characteristic emotion induced by a contact with nature—a kind of exultant melancholy which is the nearest approach to quiet unpassionate happiness that the soul can know. Happiness of whatever sort is extraordinarily hard to analyse and describe. One can think of a hundred poems, plays, and novels that deal exhaustively with pain and misery to one that is an analysis and an infectious description of happiness. Passionate joy is more easily recapturable in art ; it is dramatic, vehemently defined. But quiet happiness, which is at the same time a kind of melancholy—there you have an emotion which is inexpressible except by a mind gifted with a diversity of rarely combined qualities. The poet who would sing of this happiness must combine a rare penetration with a rare candour and honesty of mind. A man who feels an emotion that is very difficult to express is often tempted to describe it in terms of something entirely different. Platonist poets feel a powerful emotion when confronted by beauty, and, finding it a

matter of the greatest difficulty to say
precisely what that emotion is in itself,
proceed to describe it in terms of theology
which has nothing whatever to do with
the matter in point. Groping after an
expression of the emotions aroused in
him by the contemplation of nature,
Wordsworth sometimes stumbles doubt-
fully along philosophical byways that are
at the best parallel to the direct road
for which he is seeking. Everywhere in
literature this difficulty in finding an
expression for any undramatic, ill-defined
emotion is constantly made apparent.

Thomas's limpid honesty of mind saves
him from the temptation to which so
many others succumb, the temptation
to express one thing, because it is with
difficulty describable, in terms of something else. He never philosophizes the
emotions which he feels in the presence
of nature and beauty, but presents them
as they stand, transmitting them directly
to his readers without the interposition
of any obscuring medium. Rather than
attempt to explain the emotion, to
rationalize it into something that it is
not, he will present it for what it is, a
problem of which he does not know the

solution. In " Tears " we have an example of this candid confession of ignorance :

It seems I have no tears left. They should have fallen—
Their ghosts, if tears have ghosts, did fall— that day
When twenty hounds streamed by me, not yet combed out
But still all equals in their rage of gladness
Upon the scent, made one, like a great dragon
In Blooming Meadow that bends towards the sun
And once bore hops : and on that other day
When I stepped out from the double-shadowed Tower
Into an April morning, stirring and sweet
And warm. Strange solitude was there and silence.
A mightier charm than any in the Tower
Possessed the courtyard. They were changing guard,
Soldiers in line, young English countrymen,
Fair-haired and ruddy, in white tunics. Drums
And fifes were playing " The British Grenadiers."
The men, the music piercing that solitude
And silence, told me truths I had not dreamed,
And have forgotten since their beauty passed.

The emotion is nameless and indescribable, but the poet has intensely felt it and

EDWARD THOMAS

transmitted it to us who read his poem,
so that we, too, feel it with the same
intensity. Different aspects of this same
nameless emotion of quiet happiness shot
with melancholy are the theme of almost
all Thomas's poems. They bring to us
precisely that consolation and strength
which the country and solitude and
leisure bring to the spirits of those long
pent in populous cities, but essentialized
and distilled in the form of art. They
are the light that makes young again the
tattered leaves.

Of the purely æsthetic qualities of
Thomas's poetry it is unnecessary to
say much. He devised a curiously bare
and candid verse to express with all
possible simplicity and clarity his clear
sensations and emotions. . . . " This is
not," as Mr. de la Mare says in his foreword to Thomas's *Collected Poems*, " this
is not a poetry that will drug or in-
toxicate. . . . It must be read slowly,
as naturally as if it were prose, without
emphasis." With this bare verse, devoid
of any affectation, whether of clever-
ness or a too great simplicity, Thomas
could do all that he wanted. See, for
example, with what extraordinary bright-

ness and precision he could paint a
picture :

> Lichen, ivy and moss
> Keep evergreen the trees
> That stand half flayed and dying,
> And the dead trees on their knees
> In dog's mercury and moss :
> And the bright twit of the goldfinch drops
> Down there as he flits on thistle-tops.

The same bare precision served him well
for describing the interplay of emotions,
as in " After you Speak " or " Like the
Touch of Rain." And with this verse
of his he could also chant the praises of
his English countryside and the character
of its people, as typified in Lob-lie-by-
the-fire :

He has been in England as long as dove and
    daw,
Calling the wild cherry tree the merry tree,
The rose campion Bridget-in-her-bravery ;
And in a tender mood he, as I guess,
Christened one flower Love-in-idleness . . .

A WORDSWORTH
ANTHOLOGY[1]

TO regard Wordsworth critically, im-
personally, is for some of us a
rather difficult matter. With the dis-
integration of the solid orthodoxies
Wordsworth became for many intelligent,
liberal-minded families the Bible of that
sort of pantheism, that dim faith in the
existence of a spiritual world, which filled,
somewhat inadequately, the place of the
older dogmas. Brought up as children
in the Wordsworthian tradition, we were
taught to believe that a Sunday walk
among the hills was somehow equivalent
to church-going : the First Lesson was to
be read among the clouds, the Second
in the primroses ; the birds and the
running waters sang hymns, and the
whole blue landscape preached a sermon
" of moral evil and of good." From this
dim religious education we brought away
a not very well-informed veneration for
the name of Wordsworth, a dutiful conviction about the spirituality of Nature
in general, and an extraordinary superstition about mountains in particular—

[1] *Wordsworth : an Anthology*, edited, with a Preface,
by T. J. Cobden-Sanderson. R. Cobden-Sanderson.

a superstition that it took at least three seasons of Alpine Sports to dissipate entirely. Consequently, on reaching man's estate, when we actually came to read our Wordsworth, we found it extremely difficult to appraise his greatness, so many veils of preconceived ideas had to be pushed aside, so many inveterate deflections of vision allowed for. However, it became possible at last to look at Wordsworth as a detached phenomenon in the world of ideas and not as part of the family tradition of childhood.

Like many philosophers, and especially philosophers of a mystical tinge of thought, Wordsworth based his philosophy on his emotions. The conversion of emotions into intellectual terms is a process that has been repeated a thousand times in the history of the human mind. We feel a powerful emotion before a work of art, therefore it partakes of the divine, is a reconstruction of the Idea of which the natural object is a poor reflection. Love moves us deeply, therefore human love is a type of divine love. Nature in her various aspects inspires us with fear, joy, contentment, despair, therefore Nature is a soul that expresses anger, sympathy, love, and hatred. One could go on indefinitely multiplying examples of the way in which man objectifies the kingdoms of heaven and hell that are within him. The process is often a dangerous one. The mystic who feels within himself the stirrings of inenarrable emotions is not content with these emotions as they are in themselves. He feels it necessary to invent a whole cosmogony that will account for them. To him this philosophy will be true, in so far as it is an expression in intellectual terms of these emotions. But to those who do not know these emotions at first hand, it will be simply misleading. The mystical emotions have what may be termed a conduct value ; they enable the man who feels them to live his life with a serenity and confidence unknown to other men. But the philosophical terms in which these emotions are expressed have not necessarily any truth value. This mystical philosophy will be valuable only in so far as it revives, in the minds of its students, those conduct-affecting emotions which originally gave it birth. Accepted at its intellectual face value, such a philosophy may not only have no worth ; it may be actually harmful.

Into this beautifully printed volume Mr. Cobden-Sanderson has gathered together most of the passages in Words-worth's poetry which possess the power of reviving the emotions that inspired them. It is astonishing to find that they fill the best part of two hundred and fifty pages, and that there are still plenty of poems—" Peter Bell," for example—that one would like to see included. " The Prelude " and " Excursion " yield a rich tribute of what our ancestors would have called " beauties." There is that astonishing passage in which the poet describes how, as a boy, he rowed by moonlight across the lake :

And, as I rose upon the stroke, my boat
Went heaving through the water like a swan ;
When, from behind that craggy steep till then
The horizon's bound, a huge peak, black and
    huge,
As if with voluntary power instinct,
Upreared its head. I struck and struck again,
And growing still in stature the grim shape
Towered up between me and the stars, and still,
For so it seemed, with purpose of its own
And measured motion, like a living thing,
Strode after me.

There is the history of that other fearful
moment when

> I heard among the solitary hills
> Low breathings coming after me, and sounds
> Of undistinguishable motion, steps
> Almost as silent as the turf they trod.

And there are other passages telling of
Nature in less awful and menacing aspects,
Nature the giver of comfort and strong
serenity. Reading these we are able in
some measure to live for ourselves the
emotions that were Wordsworth's. If
we can feel his " shadowy exaltations,"
we have got all that Wordsworth can
give us. There is no need to read the
theology of his mysticism, the pantheistic
explanation of his emotions. To Peter
Bell a primrose by a river's brim was
only a yellow primrose. Its beauty
stirred in him no feeling. But one can
be moved by the sight of the primrose
without necessarily thinking, in the words
of Mr. Cobden-Sanderson's preface, of
" the infinite tenderness of the infinitely great, of the infinitely great which,
from out the infinite and amid its own
stupendous tasks, stoops to strew the
path of man, the infinitely little, with
sunshine and with flowers." This is

the theology of our primrose emotion. But it is the emotion itself which is important, not the theology. The emotion has its own powerful conduct value, whereas the philosophy derived from it, suspiciously anthropocentric, possesses, we should imagine, only the smallest value as truth.

VERHAEREN

VERHAEREN was one of those men who feel all their life long "l'envie" (to use his own admirably expressive phrase), "l'envie de tailler en drapeaux l'étoffe de la vie." The stuff of life can be put to worse uses. To cut it into flags is, on the whole, more admirable than to cut it, shall we say, into cerecloths, or money-bags, or Parisian underclothing. A flag is a brave, a cheerful and a noble object. These are qualities for which we are prepared to forgive the flag its over-emphasis, its lack of subtlety, its touch of childishness. One can think of a number of writers who have marched through literary history like an army with banners. There was Victor Hugo, for example—one of Verhaeren's admired masters. There was Balzac, to whose view of life Verhaeren's was, in some points, curiously akin. Among the minor makers of oriflammes there is our own Mr. Chesterton, with his heroic air of being for ever on the point of setting out on a crusade, glorious with bunting and mounted on a rocking-horse.

The flag-maker is a man of energy and

strong vitality. He likes to imagine that all that surrounds him is as large, as full of sap and as vigorous as he feels himself to be. He pictures the world as a place where the colours are strong and brightly contrasted, where a vigorous chiaroscuro leaves no doubt as to the true nature of light and darkness, and where all life pulsates, quivering and taut, like a banner in the wind. From the first we find in Verhaeren all the characteristics of the tailor of banners. In his earliest book of verse, *Les Flamands*, we see him already delighting in such lines as

Leurs deux poings monstrueux pataugeaient
    dans la pâte.

Already too we find him making copious use—or was it abuse ?—as Victor Hugo had done before him, of words like " vaste," " énorme," " infini," " infiniment," " infinité," " univers." Thus, in " L'Ame de la Ville," he talks of an " énorme " viaduct, an " immense " train, a " monstrueux " sun, even of the " énorme " atmosphere. For Verhaeren all roads lead to the infinite, wherever and whatever that may be.

VERHAEREN

Les grand'routes tracent des croix
A l'infini, à travers bois ;
Les grand'routes tracent des croix lointaines
A l'infini, à travers plaines.

Infinity is one of those notions which
are not to be lightly played with. The
makers of flags like it because it can be
contrasted so effectively with the micro-
scopic finitude of man. Writers like
Hugo and Verhaeren talk so often and
so easily about infinity that the idea
ceases in their poetry to have any meaning at all.

I have said that, in certain respects,
Verhaeren, in his view of life, is not
unlike Balzac. This resemblance is most
marked in some of the poems of his
middle period, especially those in which
he deals with aspects of contemporary
life. *Les Villes tentaculaires* contains
poems which are wholly Balzacian in
conception. Take, for example, Verhaeren's rhapsody on the Stock Exchange :

Une fureur réenflammée
Au mirage du moindre espoir
Monte soudain de l'entonnoir
De bruit et de fumée,
Ou l'on se bat, à coups de vols, en bas.
Langues sèches, regards aigus, gestes inverses,

Et cervelles, qu'en tourbillons les millions
    traversent,
Echangent là leur peur et leur terreur . . .
Aux fins de mois, quand les débâcles se décident
La mort les paraphe de suicides,
Mais au jour même aus heures blêmes,
Les volontés dans la fièvre revivent,
L'acharnement sournois
Reprend comme autrefois.

One cannot read these lines without
thinking of Balzac's feverish money-
makers, of the Baron de Nucingen, Du
Tillet, the Kellers and all the lesser misers
and usurers, and all their victims. With
their worked-up and rather melodramatic
excitement, they breathe the very spirit
of Balzac's prodigious film-scenario version
of life.

Verhaeren's flag-making instinct led
him to take special delight in all that is
more than ordinarily large and strenuous.
He extols and magnifies the gross violence
of the Flemish peasantry, their almost
infinite capacity for taking food and
drink, their industry, their animalism.
In true Rooseveltian style, he admired
energy for its own sake. All his romping
rhythms were dictated to him by the
need to express this passion for the

strenuous. His curious assonances and alliterations—

Luttent et s'entrebuttent en disputes—

arise from this same desire to recapture the sense of violence and immediate life.

It is interesting to compare the violence and energy of Verhaeren with the violence of an earlier poet—Rimbaud, the marvellous boy, if ever there was one. Rimbaud cut the stuff of life into flags, but into flags that never fluttered on this earth. His violence penetrated, in some sort, beyond the bounds of ordinary life. In some of his poems Rimbaud seems actually to have reached the nameless goal towards which he was striving, to have arrived at that world of unheard-of spiritual vigour and beauty whose nature he can only describe in an exclamatory metaphor :

Millions d'oiseaux d'or, ô future vigueur !

But the vigour of Verhaeren is never anything so fine and spiritual as this "million of golden birds." It is merely the vigour and violence of ordinary life speeded up to cinema intensity.

It is a noticeable fact that Verhaeren

was generally at his best when he took a holiday from the making and waving of flags. His Flemish bucolics and the love poems of *Les Heures*, written for the most part in traditional form, and for the most part shorter and more concentrated than his poems of violence and energy, remain the most moving portion of his work. Very interesting, too, are the poems belonging to that early phase of doubt and depression which saw the publication of *Les Débâcles* and *Les Flambeaux Noirs*. The energy and life of the later books is there, but in some sort concentrated, preserved and intensified, because turned inwards upon itself. Of many of the later poems one feels that they were written much too easily. These must have been brought very painfully and laboriously to the birth.

EDWARD LEAR

THERE are few writers whose works I care to read more than once, and one of them is certainly Edward Lear. Nonsense, like poetry, to which it is closely allied, like philosophic speculation, like every product of the imagination, is an assertion of man's spiritual freedom in spite of all the oppression of circumstance. As long as it remains possible for the human mind to invent the Quangle Wangle and the Fimble Fowl, to wander at will over the Great Gromboolian Plain and the hills of the Cnankly Bore, the victory is ours. The existence of nonsense is the nearest approach to a proof of that unprovable article of faith, whose truth we must all assume or perish miserably : that life is worth living. It is when circumstances combine to prove, with syllogistic cogency, that life is not worth living that I turn to Lear and find comfort and refreshment. I read him and I perceive that it is a good thing to be alive ; for I am free, with Lear, to be as inconsequent as I like.

Lear is a genuine poet. For what is his nonsense except the poetical imagination a little twisted out of its course ?

Lear had the true poet's feeling for words—words in themselves, precious and melodious, like phrases of music ; personal as human beings. Marlowe talks of entertaining divine Zenocrate ; Milton of the leaves that fall in Vallombrosa ; Lear of the Fimble Fowl with a corkscrew leg, of runcible spoons, of things meloobious and genteel. Lewis Carroll wrote nonsense by exaggerating sense—a too logical logic. His coinages of words are intellectual. Lear, more characteristically a poet, wrote nonsense that is an excess of imagination, coined words for the sake of their colour and sound alone. His is the purer nonsense, because more poetical. Change the key ever so little and the " Dong with a Luminous Nose " would be one of the most memorable romantic poems of the nineteenth century. Think, too, of that exquisite " Yonghy Bonghy Bo " ! In one of Tennyson's later volumes there is a charming little lyric about Catullus, which begins :

> Row us out from Desenzano,
>   To your Sirmione row !
> So they row'd, and there we landed—
>   *O venusta Sirmio !*

Can one doubt for a moment that he was

thinking, when he wrote these words, of that superb stanza with which the " Yonghy Bonghy " opens :

> On the coast of Coromandel,
>> Where the early pumpkins blow,
> In the middle of the woods,
>> Dwelt the Yonghy Bonghy Bo.

Personally, I prefer Lear's poem ; it is the richer and the fuller of the two.

Lear's genius is at its best in the Nonsense Rhymes, or Limericks, as a later generation has learned to call them. In these I like to think of him not merely as a poet and a draughtsman—and how unique an artist the recent efforts of Mr. Nash to rival him have only affirmed —but also as a profound social philosopher. No study of Lear would be complete without at least a few remarks on " They " of the Nonsense Rhymes. " They " are the world, the man in the street ; " They " are what the leader-writers in the twopenny press would call all Right-Thinking Men and Women ; " They " are Public Opinion. The Nonsense Rhymes are, for the most part, nothing more nor less than episodes selected from the history of that eternal struggle between the genius or the eccentric and his fellow-beings. Public Opinion universally abhors eccentricity. There was, for example, that charming Old Man of Melrose who walked on the tips of his toes. But "They" said (with their usual inability to appreciate the artist), "It ain't pleasant to see you at present, you stupid old man of Melrose." Occasionally, when the eccentric happens to be a criminal genius, "They" are doubtless right. The Old Man with a Gong who bumped on it all the day long deserved to be smashed. (But "They" also smashed a quite innocuous Old Man of Whitehaven merely for dancing a quadrille with a raven.) And there was that Old Person of Buda, whose conduct grew ruder and ruder; "They" were justified, I dare say, in using a hammer to silence his clamour. But it raises the whole question of punishment and of the relation between society and the individual.

When "They" are not offensive, they content themselves with being foolishly inquisitive. Thus, "They" ask the Old Man of the Wrekin whether his boots are made of leather. "They" pester the Old

EDWARD LEAR

Man in a Tree with imbecile questions
about the Bee which so horribly bored
him. In these encounters the geniuses
and the eccentrics often get the better
of the gross and heavy-witted public.
The Old Person of Ware who rode on
the back of a bear certainly scored off
" Them." For when " They " asked,
" Does it trot ? " he replied, " It does
not." (The picture shows it galloping
ventre à terre.) " It's a Moppsikon
Floppsikon bear." Sometimes, too, the
eccentric actually leads " Them " on to
their discomfiture. One thinks of that
Old Man in a Garden, who always begged
every one's pardon. When " They "
asked him, What for ? he replied,
" You're a bore, and I trust you'll go
out of my garden." But they probably
ended up by smashing him.

Occasionally the men of genius adopt
a Mallarméen policy. They flee from
the gross besetting crowd.

La chair est triste, hélas, et j'ai lu tous les
livres.
Fuir, là-bas, fuir. . . .

It was surely with these words on his
lips that the Old Person of Bazing (whose

171

presence of mind, for all that he was a Symbolist, was amazing) went out to purchase the steed which he rode at full speed and escaped from the people of Bazing. He chose the better part ; for it is almost impossible to please the mob. The Old Person of Ealing was thought by his suburban neighbours to be almost devoid of good feeling, because, if you please, he drove a small gig with three owls and a pig. And there was that pathetic Old Man of Thermopylæ (for whom I have a peculiar sympathy, since he reminds me so poignantly of myself) who never did anything properly. " They " said, " If you choose to boil eggs in your shoes, you shall never remain in Thermopylæ." The sort of people " They " like do the stupidest things, have the vulgarest accomplishments. Of the Old Person of Filey his acquaintance was wont to speak highly because he danced perfectly well to the sound of a bell. And the people of Shoreham adored that fellow-citizen of theirs whose habits were marked by decorum and who bought an umbrella and sate in the cellar. Naturally ; it was only to be expected.

SIR CHRISTOPHER WREN

THAT an Englishman should be a very great plastic artist is always rather surprising. Perhaps it is a matter of mere chance; perhaps it has something to do with our national character—if such a thing really exists. But, whatever may be the cause, the fact remains that England has produced very few artists of first-class importance. The Renaissance, as it spread, like some marvellous infectious disease of the spirit, across the face of Europe, manifested itself in different countries by different symptoms. In Italy, the country of its origin, the Renaissance was, more than anything, an outburst of painting, architecture and sculpture. Scholarship and religious reformation were, in Germany, the typical manifestations of the disease. But when this gorgeous spiritual measles crossed the English Channel, its symptoms were almost exclusively literary. The first premonitory touch of the infection from Italy " brought out " Chaucer. With the next bout of the disease England produced the Elizabethans. But among all these poets there was not a single plastic artist whose name we so much as remember.

And then, suddenly, the seventeenth century gave birth to two English artists of genius. It produced Inigo Jones and, a little later, Wren. Wren died, at the age of more than ninety, in the spring of 1723. We are celebrating to-day his bi-centenary—celebrating it not merely by antiquarian talk and scholarly appreciations of his style but also (the signs are not wanting) in a more concrete and living way : by taking a renewed interest in the art of which he was so great a master and by reverting in our practice to that fine tradition which he, with his predecessor, Inigo, inaugurated.

An anniversary celebration is an act of what Wordsworth would have called " natural piety " ; an act by which past is linked with present and of the vague, interminable series of the days a single comprehensible and logical unity is created in our minds. At the coming of the centenaries we like to remember the great men of the past, not so much by way of historical exercise, but that we may see precisely where, in relation to their achievement, we stand at the present time, that we may appraise the life still left in their spirit and apply to ourselves the moral of their example. I have no intention in this article of giving a biography of Wren, a list of his works, or a technical account of his style and methods. I propose to do no more than describe, in the most general terms, the nature of his achievement and its significance to ourselves.

Wren was a good architect. But since it is important to know precisely what we are talking about, let us begin by asking ourselves what good architecture is. Descending with majesty from his private Sinai, Mr. Ruskin dictated to a whole generation of Englishmen the æsthetic Law. On monolithic tables that were the Stones of Venice he wrote the great truths that had been revealed to him. Here is one of them :

It is to be generally observed that the proportions of buildings have nothing to do with the style or general merit of their architecture. An architect trained in the worst schools and utterly devoid of all meaning or purpose in his work, may yet have such a natural gift of massing and grouping as will render his structure effective when seen at a distance.

Now it is to be generally observed, as

he himself would say, that in all matters connected with art, Ruskin is to be interpreted as we interpret dreams—that is to say, as signifying precisely the opposite of what he says. Thus, when we find him saying that good architecture has nothing to do with proportion or the judicious disposition of masses and that the general effect counts for nothing at all, we may take it as more or less definitely proven that good architecture is, in fact, almost entirely a matter of proportion and massing, and that the general effect of the whole work counts for nearly everything. Interpreted according to this simple oneirocritical method, Ruskin's pontifical pronouncement may be taken as explaining briefly and clearly the secrets of good architecture. That is why I have chosen this quotation to be the text of my discourse on Wren.

For the qualities which most obviously distinguish Wren's work are precisely those which Ruskin so contemptuously disparages and which we, by our process of interpretation, have singled out as the essentially architectural qualities. In all that Wren designed—I am speaking of the works of his maturity; for at the beginning of his career he was still an unpractised amateur, and at the end, though still on occasion wonderfully successful, a very old man—we see a faultless proportion, a felicitous massing and contrasting of forms. He conceived his buildings as three-dimensional designs which should be seen, from every point of view, as harmoniously proportioned wholes. (With regard to the exteriors this, of course, is true only of those buildings which *can* be seen from all sides. Like all true architects, Wren preferred to build in positions where his work could be appreciated three-dimensionally. But he was also a wonderful maker of façades ; witness his Middle Temple gateway and his houses in King's Bench Walk.) He possessed in the highest degree that instinctive sense of proportion and scale which enabled him to embody his conception in brick and stone. In his great masterpiece of St. Paul's every part of the building, seen from within or without, seems to stand in a certain satisfying and harmonious relation to every other part. The same is true even of the smallest works belonging to the period of Wren's maturity. On its smaller scale and different plane, such a building as Rochester Guildhall is as beautiful, because as harmonious in the relation of all its parts, as St. Paul's.

Of Wren's other purely architectural qualities I shall speak but briefly. He was, to begin with, an engineer of inexhaustible resource ; one who could always be relied upon to find the best possible solution to any problem, from blowing up the ruins of old St. Paul's to providing the new with a dome that should be at once beautiful and thoroughly safe. As a designer he exhibited the same practical ingenuity. No architect has known how to make so much of a difficult site and cheap materials. The man who built the City churches was a practical genius of no common order. He was also an artist of profoundly original mind. This originality reveals itself in the way in which he combines the accepted features of classical Renaissance architecture into new designs that were entirely English and his own. The steeples of his City churches provide us with an obvious example of this originality. His domestic architecture — that wonderful application of classical principles to the best in the native tradition—is another.

But Wren's most characteristic quality —the quality which gives to his work, over and above its pure beauty, its own peculiar character and charm—is a quality rather moral than æsthetic. Of Chelsea Hospital, Carlyle once remarked that it was " obviously the work of a gentleman." The words are illuminating. Everything that Wren did was the work of a gentleman ; that is the secret of its peculiar character. For Wren was a great gentleman : one who valued dignity and restraint and who, respecting himself, respected also humanity ; one who desired that men and women should live with the dignity, even the grandeur, befitting their proud human title ; one who despised meanness and oddity as much as vulgar ostentation ; one who admired reason and order, who distrusted all extravagance and excess. A gentleman, the finished product of an old and ordered civilization.

Wren, the restrained and dignified gentleman, stands out most clearly when we compare him with his Italian contemporaries. The baroque artists of the seventeenth century were interested above everything in the new, the startling, the astonishing ; they strained after impossible grandeurs, unheard-of violences. The architectural ideals of which they dreamed were more suitable for embodiment in theatrical cardboard than in stone. And indeed, the late seventeenth and early eighteenth century was the golden age of scene-painting in Italy. The artists who painted the settings for the elder Scarlatti's operas, the later Bibienas and Piranesis, came nearer to reaching the wild Italian ideal than ever mere architects like Borromini or Bernini, their imaginations cramped by the stubbornness of stone and the unsleeping activities of gravitations, could hope to do.

How vastly different is the baroque theatricality from Wren's sober restraint ! Wren was a master of the grand style ; but he never dreamed of building for effect alone. He was never theatrical or showy, never pretentious or vulgar. St. Paul's is a monument of temperance and chastity. His great palace at Hampton Court is no gaudy stage-setting for the farce of absolute monarchy. It is a country gentleman's house—more spacious, of course, and with statelier rooms and more impressive vistas—but still a house meant to be lived in by someone who was a man as well as a king. But if his palaces might have housed, without the least incongruity, a well-bred gentleman, conversely his common houses were always dignified enough, however small, to be palaces in miniature and the homes of kings.

In the course of the two hundred years which have elapsed since his death, Wren's successors have often departed, with melancholy results, from the tradition of which he was the founder. They have forgotten, in their architecture, the art of being gentlemen. Infected by a touch of the baroque *folie de grandeur*, the architects of the eighteenth century built houses in imitation of Versailles and Caserta—huge stage houses, all for show and magnificence and all but impossible to live in.

The architects of the nineteenth century sinned in a diametrically opposite way—towards meanness and a negation of art. Senselessly preoccupied with details, they created the nightmare architecture of " features." The sham Gothic of early

Victorian times yielded at the end of the century to the nauseous affectation of " sham-peasantry." Big houses were built with all the irregularity and more than the " quaintness " of cottages ; suburban villas took the form of machine-made imitations of the Tudor peasant's hut. To all intents and purposes architecture ceased to exist ; Ruskin had triumphed.

To-day, however, there are signs that architecture is coming back to that sane and dignified tradition of which Wren was the great exponent. Architects are building houses for gentlemen to live in. Let us hope that they will continue to do so. There may be sublimer types of men than the gentleman : there are saints, for example, and the great enthusiasts whose thoughts and actions move the world. But for practical purposes and in a civilized, orderly society, the gentleman remains, after all, the ideal man. The most profound religious emotions have been expressed in Gothic architecture. Human ambitions and aspirations have been most colossally reflected by the Romans and the Italians of the baroque. But it is in England that the golden mean of reasonableness and decency—the practical philosophy of the civilized man—has received its most elegant and dignified expression. The old gentleman who died two hundred years ago preached on the subject of civilization a number of sermons in stone. St. Paul's and Greenwich, Trinity Library and Hampton Court, Chelsea, Kilmainham, Blackheath and Rochester, St. Stephen's Wallbrook and St. Mary Abchurch, Kensington orangery and Middle Temple gateway—these are the titles of a few of them. They have much, if we will but study them, to teach us.

BEN JONSON[1]

IT comes as something of a surprise to find that the niche reserved for Ben Jonson in the " English Men of Letters " series has only now been filled. One expected somehow that he would have been among the first of the great ones to be enshrined; but no, he has had a long time to wait; and Adam Smith, and Sydney Smith, and Hazlitt, and Fanny Burney have gone before him into the temple of fame. Now, however, his monument has at last been made, with Professor Gregory Smith's qualified version of " O rare Ben Jonson ! " duly and definitively carved upon it

What is it that makes us, almost as a matter of course, number Ben Jonson among the great ? Why should we expect him to be an early candidate for immortality, or why, indeed, should he be admitted to the " English Men of Letters " series at all ? These are difficult questions to answer; for when we come to consider the matter we find ourselves unable to give any very glowing account of Ben or his greatness. It is

[1] *Ben Jonson*, by G. Gregory Smith. (English Men of Letters Series.) Macmillan, 1919.

184

hard to say that one likes his work; one
cannot honestly call him a good poet or
a supreme dramatist. And yet, unsympathetic as he is, uninteresting as he
often can be, we still go on respecting
and admiring him, because, in spite of
everything, we are conscious, obscurely
but certainly, that he was a great man.

He had little influence on his successors;
the comedy of humours died without
any but an abortive issue. Shadwell, the
mountain-bellied " Og, from a treason
tavern rolling home," is not a disciple
that any man would have much pride in
claiming. No raking up of literary history will make Ben Jonson great as a
founder of a school or an inspirer of
others. His greatness is a greatness of
character. There is something almost
alarming in the spectacle of this formidable figure advancing with tank-like irre-
sistibility towards the goal he had set
himself to attain. No sirens of romance
can seduce him, no shock of opposition
unseat him in his career. He proceeds
along the course theoretically mapped
out at the inception of his literary life,
never deviating from this narrow way
till the very end—till the time when,

in his old age, he wrote that exquisite pastoral, *The Sad Shepherd*, which is so complete and absolute a denial of all his lifelong principles. But *The Sad Shepherd* is a weakness, albeit a triumphant weakness. Ben, as he liked to look upon himself, as he has again and again revealed himself to us, is the artist with principles, protesting against the anarchic absence of principle among the geniuses and charlatans, the poets and ranters of his age.

The true artificer will not run away from nature as he were afraid of her ; or depart from life and the likeness of truth ; but speak to the capacity of his hearers. And though his language differ from the vulgar somewhat, it shall not fly from all humanity, with the Tamerlanes and Tamer-Chams of the late age, which had nothing in them but the scenical strutting and furious vociferation to warrant them to the ignorant gapers. He knows it is his only art, so to carry it as none but artificers perceive it. In the meantime, perhaps, he is called barren, dull, lean, a poor writer, or by what contumelious word can come in their cheeks, by these men who without labour, judgment, knowledge, or almost sense, are received or preferred before him.

In these sentences from *Discoveries*

BEN JONSON

Ben Jonson paints his own picture— portrait of the artist as a true artificer— setting forth, in its most general form, and with no distracting details of the humours or the moral purpose of art, his own theory of the artist's true function and nature. Johson's theory was no idle speculation, no mere thing of words and air, but a creed, a principle, a categorical imperative, conditioning and informing his whole work. Any study of the poet must, therefore, begin with the formulation of his theory, and must go on, as Professor Gregory Smith's excellent essay does indeed proceed, to show in detail how the theory was applied and worked out in each individual composition.

A good deal of nonsense has been talked at one time or another about artistic theories. The artist is told that he should have no theories, that he should warble native wood-notes wild, that he should " sing," be wholly spontaneous, should starve his brain and cultivate his heart and spleen ; that an artistic theory cramps the style, stops up the Helicons of inspiration, and so on, and so on. The foolish and sentimental conception of the artist, to which these anti-intellectual doctrines are a corollary, dates from the time of romanticism and survives among the foolish and sentimental of to-day. A consciously practised theory of art has never spoiled a good artist, has never dammed up inspiration, but rather, and in most cases profitably, canalized it. Even the Romantics had theories and were wild and emotional on principle.

Theories are above all necessary at moments when old traditions are breaking up, when all is chaos and in flux. At such moments an artist formulates his theory and clings to it through thick and thin ; clings to it as the one firm raft of security in the midst of the surrounding unrest. Thus, when the neo-Classicism, of which Ben was one of the remote ancestors, was crumbling into the nothingness of *The Loves of the Plants* and *The Triumphs of Temper*, Wordsworth found salvation by the promulgation of a new theory of poetry, which he put into practice systematically and to the verge of absurdity in *Lyrical Ballads*. Similarly in the shipwreck of the old tradition of painting we find the artists of the present day clinging desperately to intellectual formulas as their only hope in the chaos. The only occasions, in fact, when the artist can afford entirely to dispense with theory occur in periods when a well-established tradition reigns supreme and unquestioned. And then the absence of theory is more apparent than real; for the tradition in which he is working is a theory, originally formulated by someone else, which he accepts unconsciously and as though it were the law of Nature itself.

The beginning of the seventeenth century was not one of these periods of placidity and calm acceptance. It was a moment of growth and decay together, of fermentation. The fabulous efflorescence of the Renaissance had already grown rank. With that extravagance of energy which characterized them in all things, the Elizabethans had exaggerated the traditions of their literature into insincerity. All artistic traditions end, in due course, by being reduced to the absurd; but the Elizabethans crammed the growth and decline of a century into a few years. One after another they transfigured and then destroyed every species of art they touched. Euphuism, Petrarchism, Spenserism, the sonnet, the drama—some lasted a little longer than others, but they all exploded in the end, these beautiful iridescent bubbles blown too big by the enthusiasm of their makers.

But in the midst of this unstable luxuriance voices of protest were to be heard, reactions against the main romantic current were discernible. Each in his own way and in his own sphere, Donne and Ben Jonson protested against the exaggerations of the age. At a time when sonneteers in legions were quibbling about the blackness of their ladies' eyes or the golden wires of their hair, when Platonists protested in melodious chorus that they were not in love with " red and white " but with the ideal and divine beauty of which peach-blossom complexions were but inadequate shadows, at a time when love-poetry had become, with rare exceptions, fantastically unreal, Donne called it back, a little grossly perhaps, to facts with the dry remark :

Love's not so pure and abstract as they use
To say, who have no mistress but their muse.

There have been poets who have written more lyrically than Donne, more fervently about certain amorous emotions, but not one who has formulated so rational a philosophy of love as a whole, who has seen all the facts so clearly and judged them so soundly. Donne laid down no literary theory. His followers took from him all that was relatively unimportant—the harshness, itself a protest against Spenserian facility, the conceits, the sensuality tempered by mysticism—but the important and original quality of Donne's work, the psychological realism, they could not, through sheer incapacity, transfer into their own poetry. Donne's immediate influence was on the whole bad. Any influence for good he may have had has been on poets of a much later date.

The other great literary Protestant of the time was the curious subject of our examination, Ben Jonson. Like Donne he was a realist. He had no use for claptrap, or rant, or romanticism. His aim was to give his audiences real facts flavoured with sound morality. He failed to be a great realist, partly because he lacked the imaginative insight to perceive more than the most obvious and superficial reality, and partly because he was so much preoccupied with the sound morality that he was prepared to sacrifice truth to satire ; so that in place of characters he gives us humours, not minds, but personified moral qualities.

Ben hated romanticism ; for, whatever may have been his bodily habits, however infinite his capacity for drinking sack, he belonged intellectually to the party of sobriety. In all ages the drunks and the sobers have confronted one another, each party loud in derision and condemnation of the defects which it observes in the other. " The Tamerlanes and Tamer-Chams of the late age " accuse the sober Ben of being " barren, dull, lean, a poor writer." Ben retorts that they " have nothing in them but the scenical strutting and furious vociferation to warrant them to the ignorant gapers." At another period it is the Hernanis and the Rollas who reproach that paragon of dryness, the almost fiendishly sober Stendhal, with his grocer's style. Stendhal in his turn remarks : " En paraissant, vers 1803, le *Génie* de Chateaubriand m'a semblé ridicule." And to-day ? We have our sobers and our drunks, our Hardy and our Belloc, our Santayana and our Chesterton. The dis-

BEN JONSON

tinction is eternally valid. Our personal
sympathies may lie with one or the other ;
but it is obvious that we could dispense
with neither. Ben, then, was one of the
sobers, protesting with might and main
against the extravagant behaviour of the
drunks, an intellectual insisting that there
was no way of arriving at truth except
by intellectual processes, an apotheosis
of the Plain Man determined to stand
no nonsense about anything. Ben's
poetical achievement, such as it is, is
the achievement of one who relied on no
mysterious inspiration, but on those solid
qualities of sense, perseverance, and sound
judgment which any decent citizen of
a decent country may be expected to
possess. That he himself possessed,
hidden somewhere in the obscure crypts
and recesses of his mind, other rarer
spiritual qualities is proved by the existence of his additions to *The Spanish
Tragedy*—if, indeed, they are his, which
there is no cogent reason to doubt—and
his last fragment of a masterpiece, *The
Sad Shepherd.* But these qualities, as
Professor Gregory Smith points out, he
seems deliberately to have suppressed ;
locked them away, at the bidding of his

193

imperious theory, in the strange dark places from which, at the beginning and the very end of his career, they emerged. He might have been a great romantic, one of the sublime inebriates ; he chose rather to be classical and sober. Working solely with the logical intellect and rejecting as dangerous the aid of those uncontrolled illogical elements of imagination, he produced work that is in its own way excellent. It is well-wrought, strong, heavy with learning and what the Chaucerians would call " high sentence." The emotional intensity and brevity excepted, it possesses all the qualities of the French classical drama. But the quality which characterizes the best Elizabethan and indeed the best English poetry of all periods, the power of moving in two worlds at once, it lacks. Jonson, like the French dramatists of the seventeenth century, moves on a level, directly towards some logical goal. The road over which his great contemporaries take us is not level ; it is, as it were, tilted and uneven, so that as we proceed along it we are momently shot off at a tangent from the solid earth of logical meaning into superior regions where the intel-

BEN JONSON

lectual laws of gravity have no control. The mistake of Jonson and the classicists in general consists in supposing that nothing is of value that is not susceptible of logical analysis ; whereas the truth is that the greatest triumphs of art take place in a world that is not wholly of the intellect, but lies somewhere between it and the inenarrable, but, to those who have penetrated it, supremely real, world of the mystic. In his fear and dislike of nonsense, Jonson put away from himself not only the Tamer-Chams and the fustian of the late age, but also most of the beauty it had created.

With the romantic emotions of his predecessors and contemporaries Jonson abandoned much of the characteristically Elizabethan form of their poetry. That extraordinary melodiousness which distinguishes the Elizabethan lyric is not to be found in any of Ben's writing. The poems by which we remember him— " Cynthia," " Drink to Me Only," " It is Not Growing Like a Tree "—are classically well made (though the cavalier lyrists were to do better in the same style) ; but it is not for any musical qualities that we remember them. One can understand

Ben's critical contempt for those purely formal devices for producing musical richness in which the Elizabethans delighted.

Eyes, why did you bring unto me these
    graces,
Grac'd to yield wonder out of her true
    measure,
Measure of all joyes' stay to phansie traces
      Module of pleasure.

The device is childish in its formality, the words, in their obscurity, almost devoid of significance. But what matter, since the stanza is a triumph of sonorous beauty ? The Elizabethans devised many ingenuities of this sort ; the minor poets exploited them until they became ridiculous ; the major poets employed them with greater discretion, playing subtle variations (as in Shakespeare's sonnets) on the crude theme. When writers had something to say, their thoughts, poured into these copiously elaborate forms, were moulded to the grandest poetical eloquence. A minor poet, like Lord Brooke, from whose works we have just quoted a specimen of pure formalism, could produce, in his

BEN JONSON

moments of inspiration, such magnificent lines as :

The mind of Man is this world's true dimension,
  And knowledge is the measure of the mind ;

or these, of the nethermost hell :

A place there is upon no centre placed,
Deepe under depthes, as farre as is the skie
Above the earth ; darke, infinitely spaced :
Pluto the king, the kingdome, miserie.

Even into comic poetry the Elizabethans imported the grand manner. The anonymous author of

Tee-hee, tee-hee ! Oh, sweet delight
He tickles this age, who can
Call Tullia's ape a marmosite
And Leda's goose a swan,

knew the secret of that rich, facile music which all those who wrote in the grand Elizabethan tradition could produce. Jonson, like Donne, reacted against the facility and floridity of this technique, but in a different way. Donne's protest took the form of a conceited subtlety of thought combined with a harshness of metre. Jonson's classical training inclined him towards clarity, solidity of sense, and economy of form. He stands,

as a lyrist, half-way between the Elizabethans and the cavalier song-writers;
he has broken away from the old tradition, but has not yet made himself
entirely at home in the new. At the
best he achieves a minor perfection of
point and neatness. At the worst he
falls into that dryness and dullness with
which he knew he could be reproached.

We have seen from the passage concern-
ing the true artificer that Jonson fully
realized the risk he was running. He
recurs more than once in *Discoveries*
to the same theme, " Some men to
avoid redundancy run into that [a " thin,
flagging, poor, starved " style] ; and
while they strive to have no ill-blood or
juice, they lose their good." The good
that Jonson lost was a great one. And
in the same way we see to-day how
a fear of becoming sentimental, or
" chocolate-boxy," drives many of the
younger poets and artists to shrink from
treating of the great emotions or the
obvious lavish beauty of the earth. But
to eschew a good because the corruption
of it is very bad is surely a sign of weakness
and a folly.

Having lost the realm of romantic

BEN JONSON

beauty—lost it deliberately and of set purpose—Ben Jonson devoted the whole of his immense energy to portraying and reforming the ugly world of fact. But his reforming satiric intentions interfered, as we have already shown, with his realistic intentions, and instead of re-creating in his art the actual world of men, he invented the wholly intellectual and therefore wholly unreal universe of Humours. It is an odd new world, amusing to look at from the safe distance that separates stage from stalls; but not a place one could ever wish to live in—one's neighbours, fools, knaves, hypocrites, and bears would make the most pleasing prospect intolerable. And over it all is diffused the atmosphere of Jonson's humour. It is a curious kind of humour, very different from anything that passes under that name to-day, from the humour of *Punch*, or *A Kiss for Cinderella*. One has only to read *Volpone*—or, better still, go to see it when it is acted this year by the Phœnix Society for the revival of old plays—to realize that Ben's conception of a joke differed materially from ours. Humour has never been the same since Rousseau invented humanitarianism. Syphilis and broken legs were still a great deal more comic in Smollett's day than in our own. There is a cruelty, a heartlessness about much of the older humour which is sometimes shocking, sometimes, in its less extreme forms, pleasantly astringent and stimulating after the orgies of quaint pathos and senti- mental comedy in which we are nowadays forced to indulge. There is not a pathetic line in *Volpone*; all the char- acters are profoundly unpleasant, and the fun is almost as grim as fun can be. Its heartlessness is not the brilliant, cynical heartlessness of the later Restora- tion comedy, but something ponderous and vast. It reminds us of one of those enormous, painful jokes which fate some- times plays on humanity. There is no alleviation, no purging by pity and terror. It requires a very hearty sense of humour to digest it. We have reason to admire our ancestors for their ability to enjoy this kind of comedy as it should be enjoyed. It would get very little appreciation from a London audience of to-day.

In the other comedies the fun is not so grim ; but there is a certain hardness and brutality about them all—due, of

BEN JONSON

course, ultimately to the fact that the
characters are not human, but rather
marionettes of wood and metal that
collide and belabour one another, like
the ferocious puppets of the Punch and
Judy show, without feeling the painfulness
of the proceeding. Shakespeare's comedy
is not heartless, because the characters
are human and sensitive. Our modern
sentimentality is a corruption, a softening
of genuine humanity. We need a few
more Jonsons and Congreves, some more
plays like *Volpone*, or that inimitable
Marriage à la Mode of Dryden, in which
the curtain goes up on a lady singing
the outrageously cynical song that begins :

> Why should a foolish marriage vow,
> That long ago was made,
> Constrain us to each other now
> When pleasure is decayed ?

Too much heartlessness is intolerable
(how soon one turns, revolted, from the
literature of the Restoration !), but a
little of it now and then is bracing, a
tonic for relaxed sensibilities. A little
ruthless laughter clears the air as nothing
else can do ; it is good for us, every now
and then, to see our ideals laughed at,

201   14

our conception of nobility caricatured;
it is good for solemnity's nose to be
tweaked, it is good for human pomposity
to be made to look mean and ridiculous.
It should be the great social function
—as Marinetti has pointed out—of the
music halls, to provide this cruel and
unsparing laughter, to make a buffoonery
of all the solemnly accepted grandeurs
and nobilities. A good dose of this
mockery, administered twice a year at
the equinoxes, should purge our minds
of much waste matter, make nimble our
spirits and brighten the eye to look
more clearly and truthfully on the world
about us.

Ben's reduction of human beings to a
series of rather unpleasant Humours is
sound and medicinal. Humours do not,
of course, exist in actuality; they are
true only as caricatures are true. There
are times when we wonder whether a
caricature is not, after all, truer than a
photograph; there are others when it
seems a stupid lie. But at all times a
caricature is disquieting; and it is very
good for most of us to be made uncomfortable.

CHAUCER

THERE are few things more melancholy than the spectacle of literary fossilization. A great writer comes into being, lives, labours and dies. Time passes ; year by year the sediment of muddy comment and criticism thickens round the great man's bones. The sediment sets firm ; what was once a living organism becomes a thing of marble. On the attainment of total fossilization the great man has become a classic. It becomes increasingly difficult for the members of each succeeding generation to remember that the stony objects which fill the museum cases were once alive. It is often a work of considerable labour to reconstruct the living animal from the fossil shape. But the trouble is generally worth taking. And in no case is it more worth while than in Chaucer's.

With Chaucer the ordinary fossilizing process, to which every classical author is subject, has been complicated by the petrifaction of his language. Five hundred years have almost sufficed to turn the most living of poets into a substitute on the modern sides of schools for the mental gymnastic of Latin and Greek.

Prophetically, Chaucer saw the fate that awaited him and appealed against his doom :

Ye know eke that, in form of speech is change
Within a thousand years, and wordes tho
That hadden price, now wonder nice and
    strange
Us thinketh them ; and yet they spake them so,
And sped as well in love as men now do.

The body of his poetry may have grown old, but its spirit is still young and immortal. To know that spirit—and not to know it is to ignore something that is of unique importance in the history of our literature—it is necessary to make the effort of becoming familiar with the body it informs and gives life to. The antique language and versification, so " wonder nice and strange." to our ears, are obstacles in the path of most of those who read for pleasure's sake (not that any reader worthy of the name ever reads for anything else but pleasure) ; to the pedants they are an end in themselves. Theirs is the carcass, but not the soul. Between those who are daunted by his superficial difficulties and those who take too much delight in them Chaucer finds but few sympathetic readers.

CHAUCER

I hope in these pages to be able to give a few of the reasons that make Chaucer so well worth reading.

Chaucer's art is, by its very largeness and objectiveness, extremely difficult to subject to critical analysis. Confronted by it, Dryden could only exclaim, " Here is God's plenty ! "—and the exclamation proves, when all is said, to be the most adequate and satisfying of all criticisms. All that the critic can hope to do is to expand and to illustrate Dryden's exemplary brevity.

" God's plenty ! "—the phrase is a peculiarly happy one. It calls up a vision of the prodigal earth, of harvest fields, of innumerable beasts and birds, of teeming life. And it is in the heart of this living and material world of Nature that Chaucer lives. He is the poet of earth, supremely content to walk, desiring no wings. Many English poets have loved the earth for the sake of something—a dream, a reality, call it which you will—that lies behind it. But there have been few, and, except for Chaucer, no poets of greatness, who have been in love with earth for its own sake, with Nature in the sense of something inevitably material, something that is the opposite of the supernatural. Supreme over everything in this world he sees the natural order, the " law of kind," as he calls it. The teachings of most of the great prophets and poets are simply protests against the law of kind. Chaucer does not protest, he accepts. It is precisely this accept- ance that makes him unique among English poets. He does not go to Nature as the symbol of some further spiritual reality ; hills, flowers, sea, and clouds are not, for him, transparencies through which the workings of a great soul are visible. No, they are opaque ; he likes them for what they are, things pleasant and beautiful, and not the less delicious because they are definitely of the earth earthy. Human beings, in the same way, he takes as he finds, noble and beastish, but, on the whole, wonderfully decent. He has none of that strong ethical bias which is usually to be found in the English mind. He is not horrified by the be- haviour of his fellow-beings, and he has no desire to reform them. Their char- acters, their motives interest him, and he stands looking on at them, a happy spectator. This serenity of detachment, this placid acceptance of things and people as they are, is emphasized if we compare the poetry of Chaucer with that of his contemporary, Langland, or who-ever it was that wrote *Piers Plowman.*

The historians tell us that the later years of the fourteenth century were among the most disagreeable periods of our national history. English prosperity was at a very low ebb. The Black Death had exterminated nearly a third of the working population of the islands, a fact which, aggravated by the frenzied legisla-tion of the Government, had led to the unprecedented labour troubles that cul-minated in the peasants' revolt. Clerical corruption and lawlessness were rife. All things considered, even our own age is preferable to that in which Chaucer lived. Langland does not spare denun-ciation ; he is appalled by the wicked-ness about him, scandalized at the openly confessed vices that have almost ceased to pay to virtue the tribute of hypocrisy. Indignation is the inspiration of *Piers Plowman,* the righteous indignation of the prophet. But to read Chaucer one would imagine that there was nothing in four-teenth-century England to be indignant about. It is true that the Pardoner, the Friar, the Shipman, the Miller, and, in fact, most of the Canterbury pilgrims are rogues and scoundrels; but, then, they are such " merry harlots " too. It is true that the Monk prefers hunting to praying, that, in these latter days when fairies are no more, " there is none other incubus " but the friar, that " purse is the Archdeacon's hell," and the Summoner a villain of the first magnitude; but Chaucer can only regard these things as primarily humorous. The fact of people not practising what they preach is an unfailing source of amusement to him. Where Langland cries aloud in anger, threatening the world with hell-fire, Chaucer looks on and smiles. To the great political crisis of his time he makes but one reference, and that a comic one :

So hideous was the noyse, ah *benedicite* !
Certes he Jakke Straw, and his meyné,
Ne maden schoutes never half so schrille,
Whan that they wolden eny Flemyng kille,
As thilke day was mad upon the fox.

Peasants may revolt, priests break their vows, lawyers lie and cheat, and the world in general indulge its sensual

appetites; why try and prevent them,
why protest? After all, they are all
simply being natural, they are all following the law of kind. A reasonable man,
like himself, " flees fro the pres and
dwelles with soothfastnesse." But reasonable men are few, and it is the nature
of human beings to be the unreasonable
sport of instinct and passion, just as it is
the nature of the daisy to open its eye
to the sun and of the goldfinch to be a
spritely and " gaylard " creature. The
law of kind has always and in everything
domination; there is no rubbing nature
against the hair. For

God it wot, there may no man embrace
As to destreyne a thing, the which nature
Hath naturelly set in a creature.
Take any brid, and put him in a cage,
And do all thine entent and thy corrage
To foster it tendrely with meat and drynke,
And with alle the deyntees thou canst bethinke,
And keep it all so kyndly as thou may;
Although his cage of gold be never so gay,
Yet hath this brid, by twenty thousand fold,
Lever in a forest, that is wyld and cold,
Gon ete wormes, and such wrecchidnes;
For ever this brid will doon his busynes
To scape out of his cage when that he may;
His liberté the brid desireth aye . . .

Lo, heer hath kynd his dominacioun,
And appetyt flemeth (banishes) discrescioun.
Also a she wolf hath a vilayne kynde,
The lewideste wolf that she may fynde,
Or least of reputacioun, him will sche take,
In tyme whan hir lust to have a make.
Alle this ensaumples tell I by these men
That ben untrewe, and nothing by wommen.

(As the story from which these lines are
quoted happens to be about an unfaithful wife, it seems that, in making the
female sex immune from the action of
the law of kind, Chaucer is indulging a
little in irony.)

For men han ever a licorous appetit
On lower thing to parforme her delit
Than on her wyves, ben they never so faire,
Ne never so trewe, ne so debonaire.

Nature, deplorable as some of its manifestations may be, must always and inevitably assert itself. The law of kind has
power even over immortal souls. This
fact is the source of the poet's constantly
expressed dislike of celibacy and asceticism. The doctrine that upholds the
superiority of the state of virginity over
that of wedlock is, to begin with (he
holds), a danger to the race. It en-
courages a process which we may be per-

CHAUCER

mitted to call dysgenics—the carrying on
of the species by the worst members.
The Host's words to the Monk are
memorable :

Allas ! why wearest thou so wide a cope ?
God give me sorwe ! and I were a pope
Nought only thou, but every mighty man,
Though he were shore brode upon his pan
    (head)
Should han a wife ; for all this world is lorn ;
Religioun hath take up all the corn
Of tredyng, and we burel (humble) men ben
    shrimpes ;
Of feble trees there cometh wrecchid impes.
This maketh that our heires ben so sclendere
And feble, that they may not wel engendre.

But it is not merely dangerous ; it is
anti-natural. That is the theme of the
Wife of Bath's Prologue. Counsels of
perfection are all very well when they
are given to those

That wolde lyve parfytly ;
But, lordyngs, by your leve, that am not I.

The bulk of us must live as the law of
kind enjoins.

It is characteristic of Chaucer's conception of the world, that the highest
praise he can bestow on anything is to
assert of it, that it possesses in the highest

degree the qualities of its own particular
kind. Thus of Cressida he says :

> She was not with the least of her stature,
> But all her limbes so well answering
> Weren to womanhood, that creature
> Nas never lesse mannish in seeming.

The horse of brass in the *Squire's Tale* is

> So well proportioned to be strong,
> Right as it were a steed of Lombardye,
> Thereto so *horsely* and so quick of eye.

Everything that is perfect of its kind is
admirable, even though the kind may not
be an exalted one. It is, for instance,
a joy to see the way in which the Canon
sweats :

> A cloote-leaf (dock leaf) he had under his hood
> For sweat, and for to keep his head from heat.
> But it was joye for to see him sweat ;
> His forehead dropped as a stillatorie
> Were full of plantain or of peritorie.

The Canon is supreme in the category
of sweaters, the very type and idea of
perspiring humanity ; therefore he is
admirable and joyous to behold, even as
a horse that is supremely horsely or a
woman less mannish than anything one
could imagine. In the same way it is a
delight to behold the Pardoner preaching

CHAUCER

to the people. In its own kind his charlatanism is perfect and deserves admiration :

> Mine handes and my tonge gon so yerne,
> That it is joye to see my busynesse.

This manner of saying of things that they are joyous, or, very often, heavenly, is typical of Chaucer. He looks out on the world with a delight that never grows old or weary. The sights and sounds of daily life, all the lavish beauty of the earth fill him with a pleasure which he can only express by calling it a " joy " or a " heaven." It " joye was to see " Cressida and her maidens playing together ; and

> So aungellyke was her native beauté
> That like a thing immortal seemede she,
> As doth an heavenish parfit creature.

The peacock has angel's feathers ; a girl's voice is heavenly to hear :

> Antigone the shene
> Gan on a Trojan song to singen clear,
> That it an heaven was her voice to hear.

One could go on indefinitely multiplying quotations that testify to Chaucer's exquisite sensibility to sensuous beauty and his immediate, almost exclamatory response to it. Above all, he is moved by the beauty of " young, fresh folkes, he and she " ; by the grace and swiftness of living things, birds and animals ; by flowers and placid, luminous, park-like landscapes.

It is interesting to note how frequently Chaucer speaks of animals. Like many other sages, he perceives that an animal is, in a certain sense, more human in character than a man. For an animal bears the same relation to a man as a caricature to a portrait. In a way a caricature is truer than a portrait. It reveals all the weaknesses and absurdities that flesh is heir to. The portrait brings out the greatness and dignity of the spirit that inhabits the often ridiculous flesh. It is not merely that Chaucer has written regular fables, though the *Nun's Priest's Tale* puts him among the great fabulists of the world, and there is also much definitely fabular matter in the *Parliament of Fowls*. No, his references to the beasts are not confined to his animal stories alone ; they are scattered broadcast throughout his works. He relies for much of his psychology and for much of his most vivid description on the comparison of man, in his character and appearance (which with Chaucer are always indissolubly blended), with the beasts. Take, for example, that enchanting simile in which Troilus, stubbornly anti-natural in refusing to love as the law of kind enjoins him, is compared to the corn-fed horse, who has to be taught good behaviour and sound philosophy under the whip:

As proude Bayard ginneth for to skip
Out of the way, so pricketh him his corn,
Till he a lash have of the longe whip,
Then thinketh he, " Though I prance all
    biforn,
First in the trace, full fat and newe shorn,
Yet am I but an horse, and horses' law
I must endure and with my feeres draw."

Or, again, women with too pronounced a taste for fine apparel are likened to the cat :

    And if the cattes skin be sleek and gay,
    She will not dwell in housé half a day,
    But forth she will, ere any day be dawet
    To show her skin and gon a caterwrawet.

In his descriptions of the personal appearance of his characters Chaucer makes constant use of animal characteristics.

Human beings, both beautiful and hideous, are largely described in terms of
animals. It is interesting to see how
often in that exquisite description of
Alisoun, the carpenter's wife, Chaucer
produces his clearest and sharpest effects
by a reference to some beast or bird :

Fair was this younge wife, and therewithal
As any weasel her body gent and small . . .
But of her song it was as loud and yern
As is the swallow chittering on a barn.
Thereto she coulde skip and make a game
As any kid or calf following his dame.
Her mouth was sweet as bragot is or meath,
Or hoard of apples, laid in hay or heath.
Wincing she was, as is a jolly colt,
Long as a mast and upright as a bolt.

Again and again in Chaucer's poems do
we find such similitudes, and the result
is always a picture of extraordinary precision and liveliness. Here, for example,
are a few :

Gaylard he was as goldfinch in the shaw,

or,

Such glaring eyen had he as an hare ;

or,

As piled (bald) as an ape was his skull.

CHAUCER

The self-indulgent friars are

> Like Jovinian,
> Fat as a whale, and walken as a swan.

The Pardoner describes his own preaching in these words :

> Then pain I me to stretche forth my neck
> And east and west upon the people I beck,
> As doth a dove, sitting on a barn.

Very often, too, Chaucer derives his happiest metaphors from birds and beasts. Of Troy in its misfortune and decline he says : Fortune

> Gan pull away the feathers bright of Troy
> From day to day.

Love-sick Troilus soliloquizes thus :

> He said : "O fool, now art thou in the snare
> That whilom japedest at lovés pain,
> Now art thou hent, now gnaw thin owné
>   chain."

The metaphor of Troy's bright feathers reminds me of a very beautiful simile borrowed from the life of the plants :

> And as in winter leavés been bereft,
> Each after other, till the tree be bare,
> So that there nis but bark and branches left,
> Lieth Troilus, bereft of each welfare,
> Ybounden in the blacke bark of care.

And this, in turn, reminds me of that couplet in which Chaucer compares a girl to a flowering pear-tree :

> She was well more blissful on to see
> Than is the newe parjonette tree.

Chaucer is as much at home among the stars as he is among the birds and beasts and flowers of earth. There are some literary men of to-day who are not merely not ashamed to confess their total ignorance of all facts of a " scientific " order, but even make a boast of it. Chaucer would have regarded such persons with pity and contempt. His own knowledge of astronomy was wide and exact. Those whose education has been as horribly imperfect as my own will always find some difficulty in following him as he moves with easy assurance through the heavens. Still, it is possible without knowing any mathematics to appreciate Chaucer's descriptions of the great pageant of the sun and stars as they march in triumph from mansion to mansion through the year. He does not always trouble to take out his astrolabe and measure the progress of " Phebus, with his rosy cart " ; he can record the god's movements in more general terms that may be understood even by the literary man of nineteen hundred and twenty. Here, for example, is a description of " the colde frosty seisoun of Decembre," in which matters celestial and earthly are mingled to make a picture of extraordinary richness :

Phebus wox old and hewed like latoun,
That in his hoté declinacioun
Shone as the burned gold, with streames bright ;
But now in Capricorn adown he light,
Where as he shone full pale ; I dare well sayn
The bitter frostes with the sleet and rain
Destroyed hath the green in every yerd.
Janus sit by the fire with double beard,
And drinketh of his bugle horn the wine ;
Beforn him stont the brawn of tusked swine,
And " *noel* " cryeth every lusty man.

In astrology he does not seem to have believed. The magnificent passage in the *Man of Law's Tale*, where it is said that

In the starres, clearer than is glass,
Is written, God wot, whoso can it read,
The death of every man withouten drede,

is balanced by the categorical statement found in the scientific and educational treatise on the astrolabe, that judicial astrology is mere deceit.

His scepticism with regard to astrology

is not surprising. Highly as he prizes
authority, he prefers the evidence of
experience, and where that evidence is
lacking he is content to profess a quiet
agnosticism. His respect for the law of
kind is accompanied by a complementary
mistrust of all that does not appear to
belong to the natural order of things.
There are moments when he doubts even
the fundamental beliefs of the Church :

A thousand sythes have I herd men telle
That there is joye in heaven and peyne in
    helle ;
And I accorde well that it be so.
But natheless, this wot I well also
That there is none that dwelleth in this
    countree
That either hath in helle or heaven y-be.

Of the fate of the spirit after death he
speaks in much the same style :

His spiryt changed was, and wente there
As I came never, I cannot tellen where ;
Therefore I stint, I nam no divinistre ;
Of soules fynde I not in this registre,
Ne me list not th' opiniouns to telle
Of hem, though that they witten where they
    dwelle. .

He has no patience with superstitions.
Belief in dreams, in auguries, fear of the

" ravenes qualm or schrychynge of thise owles " are all unbefitting to a self-respecting man :

> To trowen on it bothe false and foul is ;
> Alas, alas, so noble a creature
> As is a man shall dreaden such ordure !

By an absurd pun he turns all Calchas's magic arts of prophecy to ridicule :

> So when this Calkas knew by calkulynge,
> And eke by answer of this Apollo
> That Grekes sholden such a people bringe,
> Through which that Troye muste ben fordo,
> He cast anon out of the town to go.

It would not be making a fanciful comparison to say that Chaucer in many respects resembles Anatole France. Both men possess a profound love of this world for its own sake, coupled with a profound and gentle scepticism about all that lies beyond this world. To both of them the lavish beauty of Nature is a never-failing and all-sufficient source of happiness. Neither of them are ascetics ; in pain and privation they see nothing but evil. To both of them the notion that self-denial and self-mortification are necessarily righteous and productive of good is wholly alien. Both of them are apostles

of sweetness and light, of humanity and
reasonableness. Unbounded tolerance of
human weakness and a pity, not the less
sincere for being a little ironical, characterize them both. Deep knowledge of
the evils and horrors of this unintelligible
world makes them all the more attached
to its kindly beauty. But in at least one
important respect Chaucer shows himself
to be the greater, the completer spirit.
He possesses, what Anatole France does
not, an imaginative as well as an intellectual comprehension of things. Faced
by the multitudinous variety of human
character, Anatole France exhibits a
curious impotence of imagination. He
does not understand characters in the
sense that, say, Tolstoy understands them ;
he cannot, by the power of imagination,
get inside them, become what he con-
templates. None of the persons of his
creation are complete characters ; they
cannot be looked at from every side ;
they are portrayed, as it were, in the
flat and not in three dimensions. But
Chaucer has the power of getting into
someone else's character. His understanding of the men and women of whom
he writes is complete ; his slightest

character sketches are always solid and three-dimensional. The Prologue to the *Canterbury Tales*, in which the effects are almost entirely produced by the description of external physical features, furnishes us with the most obvious example of his three-dimensional drawing. Or, again, take that description in the *Merchant's Tale* of old January and his young wife May after their wedding night. It is wholly a description of external details, yet the result is not a superficial picture. We are given a glimpse of the characters in their entirety :

Thus laboureth he till that the day gan dawe,
And then he taketh a sop in fine clarré,
And upright in his bed then sitteth he.
And after that he sang full loud and clear,
And kissed his wife and made wanton cheer.
He was all coltish, full of ragerye,
And full of jargon as a flecked pye.
The slacké skin about his necké shaketh,
While that he sang, so chanteth he and craketh.
But God wot what that May thought in her
 heart,
When she him saw up sitting in his shirt,
In his night cap and with his necke lean ;
She praiseth not his playing worth a bean.

But these are all slight sketches. For full-length portraits of character we must turn to *Troilus and Cressida*, a work which, though it was written before the fullest maturity of Chaucer's powers, is in many ways his most remarkable achievement, and one, moreover, which has never been rivalled for beauty and insight in the whole field of English narrative poetry. When one sees with what certainty and precision Chaucer describes every movement of Cressida's spirit from the first movement she hears of Troilus' love for her to the moment when she is unfaithful to him, one can only wonder why the novel of character should have been so slow to make its appearance. It was not until the eighteenth century that narrative artists, using prose as their medium instead of verse, began to rediscover the secrets that were familiar to Chaucer in the fourteenth.

Troilus and Cressida was written, as we have said, before Chaucer had learnt to make the fullest use of his powers. In colouring it is fainter, less sharp and brilliant than the best of the *Canterbury Tales*. The character studies are there, carefully and accurately worked out ; but we miss the bright vividness of presentation with which Chaucer was to endow

his later art. The characters are all alive
and completely seen and understood.
But they move, as it were, behind a veil
—the veil of that poetic convention which
had, in the earliest poems, almost completely shrouded Chaucer's genius, and
which, as he grew up, as he adventured
and discovered, grew thinner and thinner,
and finally vanished like gauzy mist in
the sunlight. When *Troilus and Cressida*
was written the mist had not completely
dissipated, and the figures of his creation,
complete in conception and execution as
they are, are seen a little dimly because
of the interposed veil.

The only moment in the poem when
Chaucer's insight seems to fail him is at
the very end ; he has to account for
Cressida's unfaithfulness, and he is at a
loss to know how he shall do it. Shakespeare, when he rehandled the theme,
had no such difficulty. His version of
the story, planned on much coarser lines
than Chaucer's, leads obviously and inevitably to the fore-ordained conclusion ;
his Cressida is a minx who simply lives
up to her character. What could be
more simple ? But to Chaucer the
problem is not so simple. His Cressida is

not a minx. From the moment he first sets eyes on her Chaucer, like his own unhappy Troilus, falls head over ears in love. Beautiful, gentle, gay; possessing, it is true, somewhat " tendre wittes," but making up for her lack of skill in ratiocination by the " sudden avysements " of intuition; vain, but not disagreeably so, of her good looks and of her power over so great and noble a knight as Troilus; slow to feel love, but once she has yielded, rendering back to Troilus passion for passion; in a word, the " least mannish " of all possible creatures—she is to Chaucer the ideal of gracious and courtly womanhood. But, alas, the old story tells us that Cressida jilted her Troilus for that gross prize-fighter of a man, Diomed. The woman whom Chaucer has made his ideal proves to be no better than she should be; there is a flaw in the crystal. Chaucer is infinitely reluctant to admit the fact. But the old story is specific in its statement; indeed, its whole point consists in Cressida's infidelity. Called upon to explain his heroine's fall, Chaucer is completely at a loss. He makes a few half-hearted attempts to solve the problem, and then gives it up, falling back

CHAUCER

on authority. The old clerks say it was
so, therefore it must be so, and that's
that. The fact is that Chaucer pitched
his version of the story in a different
key from that which is found in the
" olde bokes," with the result that the
note on which he is compelled by his
respect for authority to close is completely out of harmony with the rest of
the music. It is this that accounts for
the chief, and indeed the only defect
of, the poem — its hurried and boggled
conclusion.

I cannot leave Cressida without some
mention of the doom which was prepared for her by one of Chaucer's worthiest
disciples, Robert Henryson, in some ways
the best of the Scottish poets of the
fifteenth and sixteenth centuries. Shocked
by the fact that, in Chaucer's poem,
Cressida receives no punishment for her
infidelity, Henryson composed a short
sequel, *The Testament of Cresseid*, to
show that poetic justice was duly per-
formed. Diomed, we are told, grew
weary as soon as he had " all his appetyte
and mair, fulfillit on this fair ladie "
and cast her off, to become a common
drab.

ON THE MARGIN

O fair Cresseid ! the flour and *A per se*
Of Troy and Greece, how wast thow fortunait !
To change in filth all thy feminitie
And be with fleshly lust sa maculait,
And go amang the Grekis, air and late
So giglot-like.

In her misery she curses Venus and Cupid
for having caused her to love only to
lead her to this degradation :

The seed of love was sowen in my face
And ay grew green through your supply and
grace.
But now, alas ! that seed with frost is slain,
And I fra lovers left, and all forlane.

In revenge Cupid and his mother summon
a council of gods and condemn the *A per
se* of Greece and Troy to be a hideous
leper. And so she goes forth with the
other lepers, armed with bowl and clapper,
to beg her bread. One day Troilus rides
past the place where she is sitting by the
roadside near the gates of Troy :

Then upon him she cast up both her een,
  And with ane blenk it cam into his thocht,
That he some time before her face had seen,
  But she was in such plight he knew her
  nocht,
  Yet then her look into his mind it brocht
The sweet visage and amorous blenking
Of fair Cresseid, one sometime his own darling.

He throws her an alms and the poor creature dies. And so the moral sense is satisfied. There is a good deal of superfluous mythology and unnecessary verbiage in *The Testament of Cresseid*, but the main lines of the poem are firmly and powerfully drawn. Of all the disciples of Chaucer, from Hoccleve and the Monk of Bury down to Mr. Masefield, Henryson may deservedly claim to stand the highest.